2nd **edition**

I0487791

THE PROCRASTINATOR'S BIBLE FOR FINANCIAL SUCCESS

MAJOR awards for a book that delivers MAJOR benefits now and into the future!

Build your nest egg-protect your money-create your own future

- Publisher's Choice Award

- Editor's Choice Award

- 5 STAR GOLD REVIEW from Clarion-foreword magazine

- 5 STAR REVIEW from Rebecca Reads

- 4 + Review from Mid-West Book Review

- Finalist for Literary Book of The Year from ReaderView.com

- Named "The Best Book in Financial Management" from Jean-Carpenter-Backus Award

- Finalist in finance in the INDIE book awards

www.bookworm.tv [1]

---

1   Web site powered by www.americanauthor.com

2nd Edition

THE PROCRASTINATOR'S BIBLE
FOR FINANCIAL SUCCESS

NINE ESSENTIAL STEPS FOR
PLANNING, BUDGETING, AND INVESTING

Frank J. Eberhart

iUniverse, Inc.
New York   Bloomington

THE PROCRASTINATOR'S BIBLE FOR FINANCIAL SUCCESS
NINE ESSENTIAL STEPS FOR PLANNING, BUDGETING, AND INVESTING

iUniverse books may be ordered through booksellers or by contacting:

iUniverse
1663 Liberty Drive
Bloomington, IN 47403
www.iuniverse.com
1-800-Authors (1-800-288-4677)

ISBN: 978-0-595-41198-6 (pbk)
ISBN: 978-0-595-87382-1 (cloth)
ISBN: 978-0-595-85554-4 (ebk)

Printed in the United States of America

To Family

Contents

Introduction   The Planning Process xi

Nine Steps for Financial and Estate Planning Success xii

Chapter I

Step 1:   Estate Planning Checklist. 1

                1a) Quick Reference Contact Information 3

Chapter II

Step 2:   Personal/Business Information 6

                2a) Trusts, Wills, Probate, and Executor Duties . . 15

                2b) Trust Strategy Summary. 27

                2c) Federal and State Estate Taxes. 31

                2d) Gift Taxes. 36

                2e) HR 1836 income tax changes, Rev.Proc.2006-53
                tax change web page & AMT Alternative Minimum
                Tax. 37

Chapter III

Step 3:   Personal/Business Budget 39

                3a) 529 and UGMA Accounts 45

Chapter IV

Step 4:   How Much Life Insurance Do You Need? 47

                4a) Life Insurance Calculator 50

                4b) Long-term Care Policies/Medicare/Medicaid . 52

Chapter V

Step 5:   Keeping Track of Your Investments 55

Chapter VI

Step 6:   Asset Allocation Investment Cycle and Retirement
                   Needs Analysis and Budget   59

                   6a) Retirement Budget 61

                   6b) The Impact of Withdrawal Rates on Your Money 64

Chapter VII

Step 7:   Risk and Reward Questionnaire 66

Chapter VIII

Step 8:   Understanding Your Investments 70

                   8a) Basics to Know-Calculate Returns 72

                   8b) Market, Limit, and Stop Orders 73

                   8c) The Primary Benchmarks 78

Chapter IX

Step 9:   Mutual Fund Checklist: Items You Need to Address
                   Before Investing   80

                   9a) A Little Housekeeping to Understand Your
                   Options for Fees Charged. 81

                   9b) The Mutual Fund (and Other Investments)
                   Checklist 83

Chapter X   Do It Right: Learn Before You Invest 87

                   10a) The Basics: Classification of Funds 90

                   10b) Types of Funds We See Most Often 91

                   10c) Specialty Funds, Alternative Investments
                   (Hedge Funds, Options, REITs, Index Funds, ETFs,
                   Money Managers, Reverse Mortgages, Interest Only,
                   ARM's, and Traditional Fixed Rate Mortgages . . . 94

10d) Comparing Mutual Funds, Index Funds, ETFs, Money Managers, and Annuities 102

10e) An Example of How I Manage a Client's Money 109

10f) Arbitration Alert. 112

10g) Understanding Mortgages 112

10g) Mortgage Shopping Worksheet 117

Chapter XI   All About Bonds. 119

Chapter XII   How to Choose an Adviser. 130

Chapter XIII   Did You Know? A Little Trivia 132

Chapter XIV   Quick Reference List of Web Pages. 134

Chapter XV   Summary   137

Glossary   Estate and Financial Definitions. 139

Notes   153

Introduction

The Planning Process

There is a lot to digest in today's marketplace, and investing can be confusing to anybody, especially considering the more than 15,000 mutual funds to choose from as well as options, ETFs (exchange-traded funds), fund of funds, closed end funds, fee-based or commission-based funds, managed money, hedge funds, bonds, annuities, types of mortgages, and estate planning. So with all these choices, how do you become and stay a winner as an individual investor? How do you keep track of it all?

You need a plan (in writing), knowledge, common sense, and research. You also need to define your goals and stay on top of your investments. If you understand how an investment works, you can then figure out how to invest or make sure somebody else invests the right way for you.

Developing your estate plan and understanding wills and trusts will help protect you and your family (self-employed individuals also need a succession plan). The reality is that it's never too soon or too late to develop an estate plan, start an investment savings plan, set up a budget, and establish a retirement plan to help guide you and your family toward achieving your goals. You need to take the following steps:

- Identify your life goals.
- Review where you are in relation to meeting these goals.
- Set up a plan (we make it easy in the following chapters).
- Implement your plan.
- Review your plan annually.

The first step in meeting your life goals is to develop or review your personal budget. Most individuals (and companies) are surprised when they actually complete a budget. A budget allows you to identify areas that you can adjust in your spending habits, as outlined in step 3 (your personal/business budget) and step 6a (your retirement budget). By defining your normal expenses in relation to your current net income, you can develop a good foundation for your financial plan.

Your plan should include provisions for savings, your children's education, mortgage protection, charitable gifting plans, emergency funding, educational costs, income protection, asset protection, funds for retirement, and succession (death) and other expenses. This comprehensive workbook (easy fill-in-the-blanks) will help you understand and establish financial guidelines for you and your family. You need to understand how certain investments work, how to set up your estate plan, and, looking forward, how to set up your retirement plan. Organization, preparation, and understanding investments will help educate you and your family and create a solid financial and estate foundation.

Nine Steps for Financial and Estate Planning Success

(*Note:* Read all the chapters for complete understanding of investments and strategies).

1. Estate Planning Checklist
2. Prepare your personal information/estate planning/investment asset details.
3. Prepare a detailed budget/cash flow/net worth.
4. Calculate how much life insurance you need
5. Set up a system to keep track of your investments and cost basis[1] as outlined in step 5.
6. Create a retirement budget.
7. Define your real risk tolerance or "financial DNA" (what really makes you pick investments or any type of purchase).

8. Understanding Your Investments/Basics/benchmarks/Calculate returns
9. Mutual Fund and Other Investment Checklist

Nobody really teaches us how to plan or invest when we're younger—or when we're older, for that matter. The good news is that it's never too late to learn or start. It is also a good idea to teach your children as you learn by setting up a budget, a chores list, an allowance, and a bank account for them.

In this book, I share my nine essential steps to help you achieve financial and estate planning success. These nine steps are designed to help you understand how investments work, get organized, set your estate plan in place, and put your goals into writing. Financial success doesn't just happen; it takes hard work, good organizational skills, planning, execution, review, and revision when necessary. I prefer financial *success* to financial *stress.*

Be prepared. Be informed. After all, it's your money!

TAKE YOUR FINANCES, YOUR ESTATE, AND YOURSELF TO A NEW LEVEL.

Best of luck,

Frank J. Eberhart, CEP, RFC
Web: www.bookworm.tv

Chapter I

Step 1: Estate Planning Checklist

The first item that you will need to complete is the estate planning checklist, which you will find on the next page. Plus, you should make copies of steps 1–6 for changes and updates to your plans and budgets. Put this information in a separate book for your records.

You need to have a current will or trust, establish your living wills, make provisions for executor/executrix of your estate, assign a guardian for your children (in the event of simultaneous deaths), name all beneficiaries (keep in mind named beneficiaries of your IRA/401K plans overrides your will or trust), and assign any successor trustees (like a bank trust department). Wills, which only become effective after death, and trusts should be reviewed every three to five years.

Furthermore, a will does not provide for incapacitation (the ability to make short-or long-term decisions for yourself); it becomes court appointed in which case the court makes financial decisions on your behalf. So you need proper health and investment proxies, and power of attorney for you and your spouse (each of you has one) to provide direction for and control of your financial decisions. You will also need the following:

- Safekeeping for children's and your and your spouse's original birth certificates
- Life insurance for estate taxes and living expenses for surviving spouse
- A copy of your trust or will with all proper insurance policy numbers, brokerage accounts, bank accounts, annuities, and any other investments deemed important—and a video of your wishes to leave no doubt of your intentions—with your attorney or executor
- Life insurance on children (to guarantee insurability)
- Long-term health care provisions, durable power of attorney for health and investment directives
- Adequate homeowner's insurance
- Mortgage insurance
- Umbrella policy (for additional liability coverage)

- Stocks, bonds, and mutual funds (if you own certificates, put them in street name[1] with a brokerage firm)
- Disability insurance (find out how much it covers and for how long)
- Long-term care policies
- IRA or other qualified plans—proper beneficiaries (spouse, trusts, and so on)
- Out-of-state property (find out probate rules and whether it's in trust)
- Annuities, investments
- Safe-deposit box with copies of social security numbers and birth certificates
- Business succession plan, key-man insurance, buy-sell agreements (determine who takes over in the event of your death)
- Current budget (review annually)
- Current retirement budget (review annually)
- A filing system that identifies all categories such as auto, insurance, expenses, credit cards, investments, receipts, and any other pertinent information

---

1   "Street name" means that you hold your securities and stock certificates in a brokerage account versus in your safe deposit box.

1a) Quick-Reference Contact Information

	Doctor	Pediatrician	Dentist
Name	_____	_____	_____
Address	_____	_____	_____
City, state, ZIP	_____	_____	_____
Phone	_____	_____	_____
Fax	_____	_____	_____
Pager	_____	_____	_____
E-mail	_____	_____	_____
Cell phone	_____	_____	_____

	Executor	Guardian(s)	Lawyer
Name	_____	_____	_____
Address	_____	_____	_____
City, state, ZIP	_____	_____	_____
Phone	_____	_____	_____
Fax	_____	_____	_____
Pager	_____	_____	_____
E-mail	_____	_____	_____
Cell phone	_____	_____	_____

	Accountant	Funeral director	Bank safe deposit
Name	_____	_____	_____
Address	_____	_____	_____
City, state, ZIP	_____	_____	_____
Phone	_____	_____	_____
Fax	_____	_____	_____
Pager	_____	_____	_____
E-mail	_____	_____	_____
Cell phone	_____	_____	_____

Other: School. School nurse, nursing home, hospital, broker, insurance company/agent, Cable Company, electric/gas/oil company emergency numbers, pharmacy

Chapter II

Step 2:
Personal/Business Information

The information in this chapter will help you establish guidelines for your estate. It will also help you understand the roles of executor, executrix, and guardians; summarize your investments, real estate, and other valuables; and learn what wills and trusts can do for you and your family. This information can also assist your financial adviser, accountant, and attorney for drafting your will or trust.

Section 1: Personal/business information

You

Name _____ SS#/EIN# ____-___-_____

Maiden name (if applicable) _____

Home address _____

Home phone _____ Work _____ Fax _____

E-mail _____ Work E-mail _____

Occupation _____ Employer _____

Employer address _____

Date of birth _____ Citizenship _____

Spouse

Name _____ SS#/EIN# ____-___-_____

Spouse's maiden name (if applicable) _____

Occupation _____ Employer _____

Employer address _____ Phone _____ Fax _____

Date of birth _____ Citizenship _____

Children

Name	Address	DOB	SS#	Married/chil-dren
_____	_____	_____	_____	_____
_____	_____	_____	_____	_____
_____	_____	_____	_____	_____

Make photocopies of your/spouse's/children's social security numbers and birth certificates, and put them in a safe place.

Parents

Name	Address	DOB	State or country of birth*
		SS#	Name changes
_____	_____	_____	_____
_____	_____	_____	_____

*This will help when establishing a family tree, legacies, and so on.

Grandchildren

Name	Address	DOB/SS#	Parent
_____	_____	_____	_____
_____	_____	_____	_____
_____	_____	_____	_____

Great-Grandchildren

Name	Address	DOB/SS#	Parent
_____	_____	_____	_____
_____	_____	_____	_____
_____	_____	_____	_____

Prior Marriages

You _____

Spouse _____

Obligations to provide child support, continued life insurance, health insurance, or alimony for the benefit of prior spouse or children?

$_____

Living will? Directions for health decisions   Yes ____ No ____

Have you provided health directive for life support? Yes ____ No ____

Existing will?   Yes ____ No ____

Last updated?   Date _____

Existing trusts?   Yes ____ No ____

    Are the trusts funded[2]?   Yes ____ No ____

Inherited assets:

    Did you file 706, 1040, or 1041?   Yes ____ No ____

Value of inheritance $ _____

Federal estate taxes paid $ _____

Notes _____

_____

_____

_____

Section 2: Assets

Market value	Joint/ individual	Location/ acct#	Corp/FLP/ trust
Primary residence	_____	_____	_____
Investment real estate	_____	_____	_____
Cash	_____	_____	_____
Stocks	_____	_____	_____
Bonds	_____	_____	_____
CDs	_____	_____	_____
Managed portfolios	_____	_____	_____
Stock options	_____	_____	_____
Annuities (variable/ fixed)	_____	_____	_____
Life insurance cash value	_____	_____	_____
Business interests	_____	_____	_____

2   You need to place the assets in title into the trust, home, broker accounts, bank accounts, and so on. Anything outside the trust goes to probate.

Managed trusts*	_____	_____	_____
Automobile	_____	_____	_____
Jewelry, art, antiques	_____	_____	_____
Other assets	_____	_____	_____
Grand total assets	_____		

> *Minus*
> Grand total liabilities (from section 3: Debt) –$_____
> Net worth $_____

    * Family estate trusts, investment management trusts, family limited partnerships, charitable remainder trusts, contract trusts, and so on.

Section 3: Debt

	Balance	Loan #	Lender
Primary residence	_____	_____	_____
Investment real estate	_____	_____	_____
	_____	_____	_____
	_____	_____	_____
Bank loans	_____	_____	_____
Business loans	_____	_____	_____
Credit cards	_____	_____	_____
Automobile(s)	_____	_____	_____
	_____	_____	_____
Other	_____	_____	_____

Section 4: Life Insurance

	Policy 1	Policy 2	Policy 3
Type of insurance*	_____	_____	_____
Premiums	_____	_____	_____
Owner	_____	_____	_____
Face value	_____	_____	_____
Cash value	_____	_____	_____
Beneficiaries	_____	_____	_____
	_____	_____	_____
Insurance company	_____	_____	_____
Loans	_____	_____	_____
Other	_____	_____	_____
Total:	_____	_____	_____

* Type of insurance you own: variable, term (10, 15, 20, 30 years), key-man, long-term care, disability, other.

If the insurance policy is in a trust, or has it been transferred[3] to a new owner for estate tax purposes? There are two things to remember about insurance: (1) it is taxable at face value in your estate if you have any incidence of ownership, and (2) gifting rules apply to transfers of cash values exceeding $12,000 to new owners. Anything over that

---

3   If you transfer an existing insurance policy, or any asset you have a 5-year look back from Medicaid. This is now for wills and trusts. The IRS can bring back the transferred asset and make it taxable to the estate and Medicaid can recalculate your holding or disallowance period and or claim the assets. Once you have passed the 5-year look back, Medicaid has no claim. IRS may have a claim for gift tax if it exceeded the allowable amount and you did not file form 709..

amount is subject to a 55 percent gift tax (reduced by 2010 to a top rate of 35 percent).

Section 5: Administration of Your Estate

Here are some definitions with which you should be familiar:

- *Executor/Executrix:* The person who takes your will to probate, collects the assets, orders appraisals, makes payments, and distributes the estate according to your will. This individual is personally liable for the investments. Any beneficiary has the right to sue the executor for any losses in value. Be sure you make the executor aware of this fact.
- *Trustee:* The person or individual to whom the executor entrusts the assets if there are minor children. The executor manages the money until the children reach the attained age. The successor trustee is someone other than you or your spouse. A successor trustee is needed in the event that both husband and wife die. While one or both of you are alive, you are the trustees. Some states hold the trustees liable for any losses in portfolio values; any beneficiary has the right to sue that trustee for the losses. You may consider a corporate trustee for this service.
- *Guardian:* The person or individual who will take care of your children and make decisions on their behalf until they reach attained age. If you do not make an appointment, the guardian could be the state.

	Name	Address	Relationship
Yourself			
Executor	_____	_____	_____
Trustee	_____	_____	_____
Children's guardian	_____	_____	_____
Spouse			
Executor	_____	_____	_____

Trustee   ＿＿＿＿＿＿＿   ＿＿＿＿＿＿＿   ＿＿＿＿＿＿＿
Children's   ＿＿＿＿＿＿＿   ＿＿＿＿＿＿＿   ＿＿＿＿＿＿＿
guardian

Please use the space below to provide any special instructions or requests for the above-mentioned persons in the event of simultaneous deaths.

＿＿＿＿＿＿＿＿＿＿＿＿＿＿＿＿＿＿＿＿＿＿＿＿＿＿＿＿＿

＿＿＿＿＿＿＿＿＿＿＿＿＿＿＿＿＿＿＿＿＿＿＿＿＿＿＿＿＿

Power of attorney (POA) for financial, and durable power of attorney for health care, for each of you. *

Power of attorney is necessary for deed transfers, financial decisions, and so on.

You   ＿＿＿＿＿＿＿＿＿＿＿＿＿＿
Spouse   ＿＿＿＿＿＿＿＿＿＿＿＿＿＿
Other   ＿＿＿＿＿＿＿＿＿＿＿＿＿＿

* If you or your spouse becomes incapacitated, the power of attorney allows you or your spouse to make health care and financial decisions for each other. Your will does not cover incapacitation; instead, such power is court appointed.

Section 6: Special Needs and Circumstances

You may wish to provide for your parents, children, grandchildren, and yourself.

Long-term health care policies   ＿＿＿＿＿＿＿＿＿
Special needs trust*   ＿＿＿＿＿＿＿＿＿
QTIP trusts†

Name	Address	Relationship	DOB
＿＿＿＿＿	＿＿＿＿＿	＿＿＿＿＿	＿＿＿＿
＿＿＿＿＿	＿＿＿＿＿	＿＿＿＿＿	＿＿＿＿
＿＿＿＿＿	＿＿＿＿＿	＿＿＿＿＿	＿＿＿＿

_____   _____   _____   _____

_____   _____   _____   _____

*   *Special needs trusts* are designed to provide income flow for disabled or handicapped individuals and to make sure that they are protected. The trusts also protect against creditors.

†   *QTIP (qualified terminal interest property* or "C" trust as it is sometimes referred as) trusts are generally used for previous marriages with children to help insure your assets pass to the rightful heirs or beneficiaries. The trust income goes to the surviving spouse (he or she cannot raid corpus, the principal, or hard assets unless specified). You can designate an IRA to the QTIP for income to the surviving spouse, which must be done through an independent trustee.

Special needs requirements:

_____

_____

Notes:

2a) Trusts, Wills, Probate, and Executor Duties

This section includes types of trusts, wills, and definitions with which you should be familiar. Most individuals do not realize that when they die, there are three choices for transfer of wealth:

- By law
- By contract
- By probate

Each state uses either civil or common law. *Common law* states allow assets to be split after individuals (married or not) have been living together for a certain period of time. *Civil law* recognizes the individual's private rights. Most states use common law.

Probate is a court-appointed system to oversee the direction and fair distribution of one's last wishes according to his or her will or testamentary trust.[4] Once the assets have passed through probate, which can take six months or more, they receive a step-up in cost basis and are distributed to the claims of beneficiaries. Creditors such as Medicaid have a right to property or assets before the heirs do. Probate fees vary and can be costly. The executor of the estate is also entitled to fees, most of which is based on the value of the estate.

The duties of the executor/executrix include the following:

- Read your will and expedite burial instructions. Meet with the attorney and key family members.
- Safeguard your assets before the official court appointment of executor. The listed executor/executrix of the estate needs to review all insurance, stock/bank portfolios, personal property, and any business interests, and he or she

---

4   Testamentary trusts are trusts written inside a will; the will/trust goes to probate then back to the trust.

must give notice to all accounts such as banks, credit cards, brokerage houses, insurance companies, etc.

- Petition the court for probate of your will. The executor obtains proof of beneficiaries/heirs, locates witnesses, and petitions for probate of your will. He or she also applies for all court orders in the administration of the estate (such as getting affidavit of domicile, death certificate, copies of the will or trust) and obtains court appointment for executor/ executrix status.

- Assemble and inventory all your assets, including all life insurance policies, tax waivers, and cash. In addition, he or she must inventory and appraise all household goods and remove valuables to a safe deposit; process all claims for amounts due; locate witnesses on any contested claims; arrange supervision of any business interests; collect all securities including interest and dividends; and review and manage all leases, mortgages, taxes, and real estate.

- Procure appraisal of assets and evidence of true value through proper appraisers as of the date of death.

- Administer your estate, which is governed by your will and the local probate law. You need to make estimates of cash needed to pay taxes, legacies, expenses of administration, and net distribution from probate. The executor makes sure business interests are in order including any liquidation or sale, adjusts any incomplete contracts, and evaluates all real estate and securities for sale if specified by your will or needed to raise cash.

- Prepare and pay your income tax for the year before and the year after death. You must make sure no further liability exists.

- Prepare and pay your inheritance and estate tax, and any state death, federal estate, and inheritance taxes due. He or she will handle any waivers or disclaims of property and releasing of property owned in other states, as well as file all forms and pay all taxes due.

- Settle all proper claims and send notices to creditors.

- Distribute your probated estate. You must prepare a detailed report for all receipts and disbursements, and note the date of the final account to all interested parties. After the court settles the account, the executor/executrix distributes any remaining property as directed by the court.

- Obtain final discharge after the final payment and distribution of all claims

Tip: Beneficiaries listed on your 401K, 403(b), and IRA's override your will.

You may want to have an attorney handle the probate process, because of the stress involved, the unfamiliarity of the process, and the time it takes (usually six months or more). The attorney or tax adviser can complete the tax returns. Check out fees prior to signing any agreements, including how much he or she charges for filing the taxes. Most of the information you need can be obtained by or provided to your attorney if you follow steps 1 and 2 in this workbook.

Unitrusts pay income to a beneficiary as a fixed annual percentage of the trust assets value. The percentage remains the same for the entire term of the trust agreement.

Annuity trusts pay a fixed annual amount to a beneficiary for the term of the trust.

A *nonmarital tax exclusion* transfers all the assets from your estate to your surviving spouse. It avoids estate taxes, but it is now fully taxable in the surviving spouse's estate. Plus, with the new state estate taxation, you may have to pay taxes over the state's exemption amount in the year of the death. Each state has established a table to determine what you would owe (see step 2, State Death Tax Table). A better solution, if your assets exceed the federal unified estate tax credit, may be utilizing an A/B credit shelter trust and a revocable and amendable living trust.

A *will* (inter vivos) is a legal document that administers and distributes your assets by the probate process, according to your instructions. The short term to processing your probate claim is around six months; the long term is twenty-four months or longer. It's relatively easy to contest a will, but more difficult to contest a trust. Wills do not provide direction for incapacitation; the executor for financial decisions generally becomes court appointed, which is a real hassle for heirs and beneficiaries. Wills only provide direction on death. A pour-over will pours the assets from the will into an existing trust created before the death of the testor (grantor). A pour-over will goes through the probate process.

A *testamentary trust* (inter vivos) is a trust written inside a will. The will goes to probate and then comes back to the trust. Testamentary trusts defeat the purpose of a trust and can cause other taxation or gift tax problems. Always check with your tax adviser or attorney.

Joint tenants with rights of survivorship (JTWROS) means that assets automatically pass to the other partner on death. However, the property and assets must pass through probate, and the entire amount is taxable in the surviving spouse's estate for federal estate tax. The exception is that most states have adopted their own "state death tax" with an exemption amount of $675,000. Anything over this amount is subject to taxation and must be filed in the year of the death. Check with your state to see what the rules are.

Tenancy in common means that each share of ownership passes in accordance with each co-owner's will. Each individual will be responsible for his or her share of taxation and/or gift tax. This can be a disadvantage if you wish to change ownership positions. Getting someone's name on a title or an asset is easy; getting the person's name off may not be as simple. Secondly, if you become incapacitated (can't function for yourself), financial decisions may become court appointed if you do not have the correct financial and health care proxies established.

Transfer on death (TOD) accounts are agreements between you and a brokerage or bank to transfer directly to a specified individual. On your death, the firm transfers the assets directly to the designated individual and you avoid probate. The assets receive a step-up in cost basis on the transferred assets. Most accounts require filing an inheritance claim or waiver of any amount over $25,000, if the designated individual is a Class B beneficiary (cousin, aunt, uncle, or nephew). Be sure to have proper health care and financial proxies included with your will or trust.

Transferring by contract: Examples of beneficiary contracts are trusts, annuities, life insurance policies, IRAs, and 401(k) plans. These products bypass the probate process and are referred to as beneficiary-designated products. Generally they are not subject to a gift tax or capital gains tax. Life insurance is income tax free and also estate tax free if inside a trust. Living probate is where the beneficiary becomes incapacitated at the time of your death. The issuing insurance or annuity companies may want the courts to oversee the supervision of the assets.

> *Intestate* is the state of dying without a will. In this case, your estate will go through the probate process and the courts will oversee the process of your financial affairs. This is not something you want to have happen.

An *irrevocable life insurance trust (ILIT)* or wealth replacement trust (WLT) places an insurance policy in trust, making the money income tax free and estate tax free. If the policy is written at the same time as the trust is established, there is no 3-year look-back provision for the IRS to bring the money back into the estate. Policies already issued and placed inside a trust require a three-year look-back for estate tax purposes.

A *Crummey trust* is the power of appointment given to the trust. A separate account is established for the trust. Each person writes a check from this trust for the other's insurance premium. The Crummey trust allows additions to the trust, under the gift tax exclusion, up to the number of named beneficiaries. Every year, a letter must be sent to each beneficiary giving him or her the right to withdraw cash from the trust. If a person withdraws the cash, the withdrawal may undo the trust.

An *A/B credit shelter trust* is a disclaimer trust that splits assets of individuals to take advantage of the current federal estate tax—which is $2 million each for 2006–2008, $3.5 million in 2009, and zero for 2010—if placed into the irrevocable "B trust". If you do not use the A/B trust, you have only one exemption! A gift of 35 percent still applies to anything "gifted" out of your estate over the $12,000 gift exclusion. It is generally funded at death; the surviving spouse files IRS Form 706 to activate the trust. If you fund the B trust while you're alive, it uses your current $1 million gift tax exemption and you are capped at the current federal estate tax exemption.

The *QPRT[6] (qualified personal residence trust)* is used for valuable properties you wish to transfer to heirs and keep in the family and out of your taxable estate. This is an irrevocable trust that uses the gift tax or unified credit to offset the tax burden to the beneficiaries of the property. The grantor (owner) places the property into the trust and retains the right to live in and use the property for a fixed period of time. The grantor pays a gift tax based on the value of the transferred property, discounted by the value of the retained interest—or can apply the current exemption for federal estate unified credit using the same discounted method as the gift tax. During the agreed term, the grantor pays taxes and mortgages and treats the property as his or her own. At the end of the term, the trust terminates and the residence or property passes to the

6   Not taken into account the actual value of QPRT or any portion of taxation used while funding the QPRT

beneficiaries named in the trust, or it continues in trust for the beneficiaries' benefit. If the grantor exceeds the term of the contract, the IRS
requires that he must rent it at fair market value, which also removes
money from the grantor's estate. If the grantor outlives the term, he
will have transferred the property out of the taxable estate including
any appreciation. If he does not outlive the specified term, the property
will come back into the taxable estate. Check with your tax adviser and
attorney for all the rules and whether they would benefit you and your
family.

In *grantor-retained income trusts*, the grantor retains the use of income
from property for a specified period of time. Provided the grantor outlives the specified term, the grantor can give away the assets at a discounted value. The value is based on the time of the gift less the value of
the grantor's retained interest. If the grantor does not outlive the term,
the assets are taxable in the grantor's estate.

A *QDOT (qualified domestic trust)* is designated for a nonresident
spouse of a U.S citizen the trustee spouse must be a U.S. citizen to qualify. The surviving spouse receives income from the trust, but for estate
tax purposes, the IRS does not want the money to leave the United
States before the death of the second spouse. The trust must have an
EIN (taxpayer identification number). If you become a U.S. citizen, you
must notify the IRS and the trust terminates. For the federal estate tax,
you must file IRS Form 706QDT.

A *disclaimer trust* is a trust in a will that leaves assets to the surviving
spouse. Generally it is used to substitute for a credit shelter trust and
take advantage of the unified credit when only a single will is in effect.
The trust only becomes effective when the surviving spouse "disclaims"
some or all the property or assets left to the surviving spouse. The IRS
rules that the disclaiming person never owned or received the property
or asset. It passes to the next recipient or beneficiary and is not federally
taxed. The surviving spouse has nine months from the date of death to

disclaim the transferred assets. You must check with your state for state death taxes that may be due.

Defective grantor trusts are designed for the benefit of your family. The donor pays taxes on all income to the trust, which reduces the donor's taxable estate. By paying taxes on all income to the trust, you are making gifts to the family, which, under current law, is gift and estate tax free. If you sell an asset, you pay capital gains tax on the profit; if you sell the asset to the trust; there is no gain to pay. The trust would pay for the assets by installment to the seller, funded by the income generated in the trust. All future assets and growth are removed from your taxable estate for your family's benefit. If you no longer pay the income taxes, you relinquish all rights of income, and the trust or beneficiaries would pay the taxes.

Special needs trusts are irrevocable trusts established for the benefit of individuals who cannot take care of themselves. They are generally funded with life insurance. On the donor's death, the life insurance proceeds are placed in trust to provide income for the special needs individual. Most states make trust document review mandatory and must approve the trust before it can be established (to avoid Medicaid abuse). Medicaid may lay claims against the trust for any funds it paid up to the donor's death.

An *LLC (limited liability company)* is generally used for individuals who have income properties. It protects against suits from renters who may be injured. You should establish an LLC for each property you own. If all properties are under one LLC, and a plaintiff files a lawsuit against one property and wins, the plaintiff has access to everything inside the LLC. With separate LLCs, a plaintiff would need to sue each one. If you place your personal residence in an LLC, you have protection, but you lose the $500,000 exemption ($250,000 for each person) on the sale for capital gains tax purposes.

Family limited partnerships (FLPs) are designed for families who wish to keep their businesses in the family. The IRS allows discounts for stock and assets to be distributed to family members. The IRS has issued many Technical Advice Memorandums disallowing excessive valuation discounts. As a general rule, the IRS requires that the value must be 70 percent of fair market value as determined by an independent appraiser. Gifting to family members uses the current gift tax exemption of $12,000. So if you gifted stock using the $12,000 current allowable exemption at 70 percent fair market value, you would use only $8,400. As you see, you could gift a lot more FLP units using this formula without violating the gifting rules. The IRS may challenge an owner's willingness to really sell his or her interest for that amount.

A *2503(c) trust,* for those who do not want a 529 or self-directed broker account (UGMA/UTMA, is a trust established for the benefit of a minor. The income can be paid out or accumulated. Income that is accumulated is taxed to the trust. The trust pays the highest income taxes very quickly. If the income is paid out, it is taxable to the minor. Any gifts to the trust must qualify for the annual exclusion, currently at $12,000 per year per individual donor. All principal and income must be made available to the minor at attained age[7] of the state in which you reside or no later than age 21.

Charitable remainder trusts (CRTs) remove assets from your estate, produce lifetime income, and receive a tax deduction based on your age at the time of the gift. In most cases, you are exchanging highly appreciated assets such as stocks, bonds, mutual funds, and real estate, which have a low cost basis so that you defer capital gains tax. In addition, after both spouses are deceased, your selected charities receive the balance of funds. Never let those charities know they have been selected, as you could change your mind. To protect the assets for heirs and beneficiaries, set up a wealth replacement trust (irrevocable life insurance trust or

---

[7]   Attained age is when a minor becomes an adult and is entitled to the assets that have been gifted to him or her.

ILIT) to replace the money that went to charity. The money that your heirs receive is income tax free and estate tax free. All charities must meet the qualifications of IRS section 501(c)(3) and pass the 5 percent probability test, which means the donation must retain at least 5 percent of corpus after the calculations for income distributions to the donor.

The two types of CRTs, for those who are charitably inclined, are as follows:

- *Fixed annuity trusts* (CRATs[8]) provide a fixed dollar amount equal to at least 5 percent of the assets placed into the trust. No additional contributions are allowed. The CRAT provides a predictable cash flow, and income must be paid out each year.

- *Variable unitrusts* (CRUTs[9]) provide income based on a fixed percentage, usually 5 percent of the assets, and must be revalued annually. Additional contributions are allowed. Your cash flow rises or falls with the annual evaluation and additional contributions. You are not required to pay out income each year.

- *Net income charitable remainder unitrusts (NIMCRUTs)* are designed for individuals who do not currently need the income. Additional contributions are usually planned. Investments can include rent, dividends, royalties, stocks, bonds, mutual funds, or real estate.

Private and Public Foundations

The IRS allows two types of charity classifications: private and public foundations. Public foundations or public charities are large publicly supported organizations. Private foundations are required to apply

---

8   Charitable Remainder Annuity Trust
9   Charitable Remainder Uni-trust

for exempt status from the IRS before they can contribute and become exempt from federal income tax.

The requirements for IRS approval status for private foundations are as follows:

- The foundation must spend at least 85 percent of its adjusted net income or minimum investment return (whichever is less) directly on its primary activities that are exempted and approved by IRS code.

- The donor can contribute up to 50 percent of his adjusted gross income.

- The foundation must file Form 1023 (recognition of exemption).

- The foundation must file Form 8718 (user fee letter request).

- The foundation must file Form SS-4 (tax ID number).

- The foundation must file duplicate originals of the articles of incorporation with the state. The secretary of state records the copies with the local registrar of deeds and issues a Certificate of Incorporation in accordance with the applicable corporate law. The foundation uses IRS Form 990-PF or IRS Form 5227 for the annual return.

- When the foundation is incorporated, it can start business and elect the board of directors.

- The donor can control the foundation but cannot engage in self-dealing, which includes making loans, excessive compensation, purchases or sales, or diversions of income to any disqualified persons. The donor must avoid investments of a speculative nature that would jeopardize the purpose of the foundation.

The combined holdings of the private foundation and all disqualified persons generally may not exceed 20 percent of the voting control in any corporation conducting business that is not substantially related to the exempt purpose of the foundation.

Web pages to assist for planned giving are as follows:
* www.giftlaw.net
* www.charitynavigator.org
* www.crescendointeractive.com

A *revocable and amendable living trust (RLT)* is a legal entity that holds or manages the assets for an individual. The grantor is the individual transferring the assets to the trust. As a general rule, both spouses are the trustees and the beneficiaries, and they outline the terms of the trust. You should also fund the trust, which consists of titling the assets in the name of the trust (i.e., John Doe revocable and amendable living trust). These assets could include a house, broker accounts, bank accounts, etc. Anything left outside the trust goes to probate. You need to obtain a trust tax ID# and use IRS Form 1041, marked grantor trust; this means there are no tax consequences, so taxable income is attributed to the grantor resulting in paying tax on such income go to the grantor. RLTs bypass probate though you still need to file in the county in which you reside and pay the probate fee. The assets inside the trust step up the cost basis on death and also transfer more easily to the surviving spouse, or any beneficiary.

In addition, you need to have a durable power of attorney for health and investment directions; A/B credit shelter trusts; a living will, which indicates what to do if you are sick, terminally ill, etc.; and power of attorneys for you and your spouse. Like a will, RLTs have no impact until death.

Here are examples of what can go into an RLT:

- Stocks
- Bonds
- Mutual funds
- Brokerage accounts
- Variable annuities
- Life insurance (taxable at face value unless in an irrevocable life insurance trust or ILIT)
- Art and collectibles
- Personal possessions
- Capital-managed accounts
- Real estate

Here are examples of what cannot go into an RLT:

- IRAs
- Pensions
- 401(k) accounts
- 403(b) and other qualified plans

You can make the beneficiary the revocable trust, and the trust can then be distributed to named beneficiaries.

2b) Trust Strategy Summary

Let's put together a strategy using trusts. You know what your net worth is from completing steps 1 and 2 of the workbook. Let us assume your combined net estate is worth $6 million, or use your actual net worth. The goal is to minimize estate and state death taxes, provide income for you and your spouse, pass the maximum amount of assets to your children, and keep the primary residence in the family. Let's say you have children from another marriage.

To help meet your goals, you do the following:

- Establish a revocable and amendable living trust (RLT) for you and one for your spouse; title assets (stocks, bonds, mutual funds, cash, real estate, broker/bank accounts) in the trust name, with a federal tax ID# and schedule A called "funding the trust"; and you file IRS Form 1041 for trusts (marked grantor trust).

- Create an A/B credit shelter trust to take advantage of the current federal estate tax exemption. The B trust is set up to provide income for the surviving spouse (the B trust could also provide invasion of the corpus to provide maintenance, education & health), and the assets upon death will receive a full step-up in cost basis on the death of the spouse, which means if you sell any assets the cost basis is from the date of death. For example, you buy a house for $100,000 and it is now worth $500,000. You sell it for $500,000 so there is no capital gain to pay. The same holds true for all assets titled such as stocks, bonds, etc., to the deceased spouse's revocable trust.

- Establish a QTIP (qualified terminal interest property) trust, used primarily for prior marriages (similar to a pre-nuptial agreement), to protect assets that are designated for your children. It provides income for your spouse, but the spouse cannot raid the corpus (assets of the trust) unless you provide access to corpus.

- Set up separate durable and medical power of attorney's for you and your spouse so you can make elective choices for health care and investment directives for each other, and establish guardianship for children or other individuals who are in your care in the event of simultaneous deaths.

- Because your primary residence is worth $2 million, you also establish a 10-year QPRT (qualified personal residence trust) to keep the home in the family (see "trusts" for a detailed explanation) and to remove it from your taxable estate.

- Because your vacation home in Florida is worth $1 million and is titled to the trust, you establish a trust. Even if you only have a will it may behoove you to establish a trust for any out of state property, especially Florida, California, or New York. If you do not, you have probate in the other state as well as probate in the state of domicile (the one you live in).

- You set up life insurance worth a face value of $5 million. You have also placed the insurance policy in an ILIT. Otherwise, the insurance would be income tax free, but taxed at face value for estate tax purposes.

- You and your spouse are each gifting $12,000 per year (current gift tax exemption) to each of your children and grandchildren. Each person can gift $12,000 per year to anybody.

Why would I use a trust versus a will if my estate is not big enough?

- Revocable trusts bypass probate though you still need to file in the county in which you reside and pay the probate fee. Like a will, you set the table for what you want to happen upon death. Anybody can contest a will because they are public. You can go the courthouse and look up just about anybody. Trusts are private and very difficult to contest.

- Revocable trusts are considered revocable grantor trusts, meaning the tax goes to the grantor (you) not the trust, and so nothing changes at tax time.

- All assets inside the trust take an immediate step-up in basis upon death of the donor (you), and the timeframe is usually less than 60 days to pass the assets to the surviving spouse or designated beneficiaries. IRS likes each of you to have an RLT, check the sunset rules for capital gains tax changes under 2d) GIFT TAX. Unlike wills and testamentary trusts (a trust written inside a will) which are designed to go to probate which can take 6 months or longer.

- If you have children, or out-of-state properties, you should have a revocable trust, and have appointed guardianship for your children in the event of simultaneous deaths, and complete durable and medical power of attorney's for each of you (you should do this even if you only have a will). The power of attorney is important because if you become incapacitated, the power of attorney for your spouse allows him or her to make decisions without court appointment. Wills do not allow for incapacitation as they only become effective on death.

- A complete set of RLT, power of attorney's, A/B credit shelter trust, and an ILIT should cost around $2,000-$3,500, which is about the same for a will with all the attachments. Watch out for cookie cutter templates-they may contain information or wordage that is not pertinent to you, or may be even potentially harmful.

  Tip: RLT's and assets transferred to the revocable trust does not remove the "transfer of asset" from the claims of Medicaid or the 5-year look back. Check with your attorney on proper Medicaid planning trusts.

Simplified Summary of Net Effect for Estate	
Liquid assets	$3 million
The primary residence from the estate[8]	$2 million
Total:	5 million
Minus current federal estate tax exemption	($4 million)
Add the life insurance from the ILIT ($5 million)	5 million
Net to beneficiaries	6 million

Established income from the QTIP for your spouse based on current value of dollar assets. Assuming you lived past the ten-year QPRT, then died, the results would be the following: $6 million tax-free has gone to your QTIP to provide income for your spouse. You've kept your primary residence in the family, and on your spouse's death, the assets will pass to your intended or specified beneficiaries and heirs, according to your final trust wishes. You have insured the passing of your estate without probate, kept control through the use of trusts, paid zero federal estate taxes, and have enough cash or liquid assets to pay for any state death taxes and final expenses.

There are many other trusts available. Always check with your tax adviser and attorney for the current rules of probate, trusts, federal and state death taxes, and how your individual estate may be affected. Be prepared! Visit www.irs.gov for more information.

2c) Federal and State Estate Taxes

The Temporary Tax Relief Bill, known as HR 1836, went into effect in 2002 and terminates in 2011. In 2011, the "sunset provision" goes into effect. This means that anything that was subject to the estate tax before 2002 will be subject to it again as follows: $1 million federal exemption for each spouse[11], 55 percent estate tax rate over the exemption amount, 35 percent cap for the gift tax. There is pressure to eliminate the federal estate death tax; most likely, there will be a compromise of higher exclusions for federal taxation. What does all that mean?

If you die in 2010, your federal estate tax is zero. If you die in 2011 or beyond, and your net estate is worth $5 million, you would pay $5 million minus the $2 million exemption (if in the A/B trust), which leaves $3 million taxed at 55 percent. In the end, you would write the IRS a check for around $1.65 million. If your net estate is worth $2 million, your tax would be zero if you have the A/B trust. Or, if you do not use the A/B trust, your tax would be $2 million minus $1 million, and the IRS would receive a check for $550,000.

You could still have state death taxes in the year of a spouse's death since those taxes are now separate from federal. The state death tax no longer "piggybacks" the federal estate tax, and each state has adopted its own death tax. The federal estate tax is due at the second spouse's death, and the current estate tax is applied to the current net value of the estate at the time of the second spouse's death minus the applied tax credit from the B trust. State death taxes over the allowable exemption may be due in the year of the first spouse's death, and any balance is due on the second spouse's death.

The state death tax table on the next page is probably more important than the federal estate tax table, which is on the page after the state death tax table. This is because most individuals never pay federal estate taxes, but they may owe state death taxes based on the exemption amount imposed by each state. Most are payable within nine months from the death of a spouse.

For example, if you live in New Jersey, which has the highest state death tax, your estate is worth $2 million and you have the A/B credit shelter trust, your federal taxation would be zero based on the current

---

11   The exemption is for each. If you don't place the spousal exemption of $1 million into the B or credit shelter trust one of the exemptions goes away. So if you or your spouse die and do not have the exemption, you would receive only one exemption.

exemption of $2 million ($1 million for each spouse). However, you would owe the difference between the New Jersey state exemption of $675,000[12] and the estate of $2 million, or around $100,000. Plus the amount is due nine months after a spouse's death. The federal exemption, if nothing changes from 2011 and beyond, will be $1 million per individual. In 2010, there are no federal estate taxes due with the death of a spouse—*not* gift tax or state death taxes. You can see the current federal estate tax rates at www.irs.gov; look for Publication 950.

In the example that follows, there is a $2 million net worth estate and the 2011 current $1 million each federal estate tax exemption. The second spouse is also deceased.

A trust (surviving spouse)	Placed $1 million federal exemption
	in irrevocable B trust (deceased spouse)
Net taxable estate	$2,000,000
Transferred from B trust to A trust	
2011 federal exemption	-$1,000,000
A trust exemption applied	-$1,000,000
Federal taxable estate	$0

Here's the example without the A/B credit shelter trust:

Net estate	$2,000,000
Federal estate tax exemption	-$1,000,000
Taxable estate	$1,000,000
Estate tax due at 55%	$550,000

---

12   Consult your tax adviser to establish your estate net worth, and be prepared to pay the state death taxes from a reserve fund.

An example with 2011 federal estate tax exemption of $1 million each, a $2 million life insurance in trust, and both spouses are deceased:

Net estate $5,000,000	Placed $1 million in irrevocable B trust on death of first spouse
2011 exemption from A trust	-$1,000,000
2011 exemption applied from B trust	-$1,000,000
Net taxable estate	$3,000,000
Federal estate tax due at 55%	$1,650,000
Proceeds from life insurance trust	$2,000,000
Net tax-free proceeds to family income and estate	$5,350,000

Here's an example without the A/B credit shelter trust and no life insurance:

Net estate	$5,000,000
2011 federal estate tax exemption	-$1,000,000
Net taxable estate	$4,000,000
Estate tax due at 55%	$2,200,000
Net proceeds to family after estate taxes	$2,800,000

The above examples do not include any state death taxes that may be due, or politicians.

State Death Tax Table

Taxable estate	Tax rate
$40,000 to $90,000	$0 plus .08% of excess over $40,000
$90,000 to $140,000	$400 plus 1.6% of excess over $90,000
$140,000 to $240,000	$1,200 plus 2.4% of excess over $140,000
$240,000 to $440,000	$3,600 plus 3.2% of excess over $240,000
$440,000 to $640,000	$10,000 plus 4% of excess over $440,000
$640,000 to $840,000	$18,000 plus 4.8% of excess over $640,000
$840,000 to $1,040,000	$27,600 plus 5.6% of excess over $840,000
$1,040,000 to $1,540,000	$38,800 plus 6.4% of excess over $1,040,000
$1,540,000 to $2,040,000	$70,800 plus 7.2% of excess over $1,540,000
$2,040,000 to $2,540,000	$106,800 plus 8% of excess over $2,040,000
$2,540,000 to $3,040,000	$146,800 plus 8.8% of excess over $2,540,000
$3,040,000 to $3,540,000	$190,800 plus 9.6% of excess over $3,040,000
$3,540,000 to $4,040,000	$238,800 plus 10.4% of excess over $3,540,000
$4,040,000 to $5,040,000	$290,800 plus 11.2% of excess over $4,040,000
$5,040,000 to $6,040,000	$402,800 plus 12% of excess over $5,040,000
$6,040,000 to $7,040,000	$522,800 plus 12.8% of excess over $6,040,000
$7,040,000 to $8,040,000	$650,800 plus 13.6% of excess over $7,040,000
$8,040,000 to $9,040,000	$786,800 plus 14.4% of excess over $8,040,000
$9,040,000 to $10,040,000	$930,800 plus 15.2% of excess over $9,040,000
$10,040,000 +	$1,082,000 plus 16% of excess over $10,040,000

Inheritance taxes also play an important role for tax collection. Class B beneficiaries pay inheritance taxes from an estate; class A beneficiaries do not.[12]

---

12   Class A beneficiary examples: mother, husband, wife, or son. Class B beneficiary examples: cousin, aunt, or nephew. Check with your state to see what the percentage tax would be.

Federal Estate Death Tax Table
(abbreviated version from 2004–2011 and beyond):

Year	Federal unified credit	Federal tax rate
2004	$1,500,000	
	48% over exemption	
2005	$1,5000,000	47%
2006	$2,000,000	46%
2007	$2,000,000	45%
2008	$2,000,000	45%
2009	$3,500,000	45%
2010	estate taxes repealed gift tax* is	35%
2011†	$1,000,000	55%

    *   Be careful, and don't be confused by the elimination of the estate tax repeal in 2010. The gift tax at 35 percent over the allowable gifting provision (currently at $12,000 per year) still applies.

    †   In 2011, the sunset provision goes into effect unless Congress eliminates, extends, or modifies the estate tax. Estate taxes will revert back to the original amounts, including a 5 percent surcharge on estates over $10 million.

2d) Gift Taxes

The current gifting provision is $12,000 ($24,000 for a married couple) per year to any individual you wish, with no tax consequences. You file gift tax returns on IRS Form 709. You can amend prior year returns if both you and your spouse are alive. The gift tax is applied from the date of the gift. In addition, the IRS allows an additional life-time gift tax exemption in the amount of $1 million, which you can take all in one year, without taxation; it reduces your federal estate tax credit by the amount you use. All gift tax returns are due by April 15. The gift tax is now 46 percent for the amount in excess of the current 2006 exemption of $12,000 per person. It piggybacks the same rate as the federal estate tax exemption and reduces to 45 percent from 2007–

2009, and it remains at 35 percent from 2010 and beyond. The carryover capital gains tax goes into effect in 2010; the first $1.3 million is exempt from taxation of the estate to a nonspouse, and an additional $3 million applies to a spouse. Anything over this amount will now be subject to long-term capital gains tax. We traded this for the lower income tax rates. *You must keep track of your cost basis* for all assets because the IRS will require this going forward. Use step 5: keeping track of your investments worksheet.

2e) HR 1836 income tax changes, Rev.Proc.2006-53 tax change web page & AMT Alternative Minimum Tax

To finish HR 1836, the income tax rates for individuals are currently as follows:

- The first $6,000 of taxable income for singles is at 10 percent (adjusted to $7,000 after 2007 and beyond), and 15 percent of the amounts over $6,000.

- The first $12,000 of income for married couples filing jointly ($14,000 after 2007) is taxable at 10 percent. All remaining portions above $12,000 of income will be taxed at 15 percent. The rest of the regular income tax rates are as follows: 15, 25, 28, and 33 percent, with the top rate now at 35 percent.

- Go to www.irs.gov type and under search type the following: Rev.proc.2006-53 or IR-2006-173 for complete information on all the tax changes now in effect for 2007.

- Contributions to 529 plans, 401(k) plans, IRAs, and Roth IRAs, including make-up provisions for people over 50, have been extended beyond 2011.

The *alternative minimum tax (AMT)* was initiated under the Tax Reform Act of 1986. It was designed to make sure high net worth individuals paid their fair share of income taxes. What AMT actually does is eliminate dollar-for-dollar tax deductions. The problem now is inflation. The regular income tax brackets, exemptions, and standard deductions are adjusted annually for inflation but the AMT brackets are not. Every year, more families are subject to the AMT:

- If you have incomes over $75,000 and have children
- If you high personal write-offs like second mortgages stock options, rental properties, S corporation stock, or partnership interests
- If you have large capital gains

Your tax adviser needs to run the comparisons for both tax systems, regular and AMT. If the IRS audits you and you have AMT owed under the AMT system, you could be liable for penalties, interest, and any back taxes under the AMT rule-the IRS does not accept "I did not know". Go to www.irs.gov and look under AMT for current rule or temporary adjustments.

Chapter III

Step 3: Personal/Business Budget

In this chapter we will identify spending habits, which will help you to make necessary changes. I have included sections for monthly amounts as well as for annualizing your expenses, and also one for income so you can see your total expenses and your total income to give you your net spendable income. This will help you to adjust your investment and retirement dollar allocations.

I think it is just as important to understand what you *owe* as it is to understand what you *own* and where it is.

Budget worksheet

	Monthly	Annually
Mortgage or rent		
First mortgage or rent	_____	_____
Second mortgage	_____	_____
Property 2	_____	_____
Property 3	_____	_____
Homeowner's insurance	_____	_____
Other	_____	_____
(Flood insurance, umbrella policy, etc.)		
Subtotal	_____	_____

Real estate taxes

Property 1   _____   _____
Property 2   _____   _____
Property 3   _____   _____
Other   _____   _____
Subtotal   _____   _____

Utilities

Gas and electric   _____   _____
Water and garbage   _____   _____
Telephone   _____   _____
Cable TV   _____   _____
Internet/ISP   _____   _____
Other   _____   _____
Subtotal   _____   _____

Insurance premiums

Life insurance 1   _____   _____
Life insurance 2   _____   _____
Life insurance 3   _____   _____
Disability insurance   _____   _____
Medical   _____   _____
Dental   _____   _____
Other   _____   _____
(Long-term care policies, etc.)
Subtotal   _____   _____

Savings/investments

Bank accounts   _____   _____

Credit union   _____   _____
CDs   _____   _____
Stocks   _____   _____
Bonds   _____   _____
College funds/529 plans   _____   _____
(See step 3a)
Annuities   _____   _____
Other   _____   _____
Subtotal   _____   _____

Education

Tuition and books   _____   _____
(Private school, college, etc.)
Lunch   _____   _____
Childcare   _____   _____
(Special needs, day care, etc.)
Other   _____   _____
Subtotal   _____   _____

Transportation

Auto payment 1   _____   _____
Auto payment 2   _____   _____
Gas   _____   _____
Insurance   _____   _____
Maintenance   _____   _____
Licenses   _____   _____
Registrations   _____   _____
Tolls/parking   _____   _____
Other   _____   _____
Subtotal   _____   _____

Charge accounts

Visa/MasterCard   _____   _____

American Express   _____   _____

Discover Card   _____   _____

Other   _____   _____

Subtotal   _____   _____

Loan payments

Loan 1   _____   _____

Loan 2   _____   _____

Other   _____   _____

Subtotal   _____   _____

Food   _____   _____

Subtotal   _____   _____

Clothing   _____   _____

Subtotal   _____   _____

Other

Travel/vacation   _____   _____

Dining   _____   _____

Contributions   _____   _____

Dues/subscriptions   _____   _____

Charitable gifts   _____   _____

Other   _____   _____

Subtotal   _____   _____

Total expenses   _____   _____

It never seems significant until you see it in writing and annualized.

Income and Expenses

	Monthly	Annually
Income		
Gross salary 1	_____	_____
Gross salary 2	_____	_____
Rental income	_____	_____
Dividends	_____	_____
Interest	_____	_____
Capital gains	_____	_____
Commissions	_____	_____
Bonus	_____	_____
Other	_____	_____
Subtotal	_____	_____
Reductions		
Federal taxes	_____	_____
State/local taxes	_____	_____
FICA	_____	_____
Social security	_____	_____
Medicare tax	_____	_____
401(k)	_____	_____
Other	_____	_____
Subtotal	_____	_____
Total net income	_____	_____

Minus
Total expenses   _____   _____

Equals
Net cash available for savings $ $
                                            _____   _____

3a) 529 and UGMA Accounts

Major Benefit Highlights:

529 money can be used for any qualified higher education expense-tuition, fees, books, supplies, computers, room and board

Change the beneficiary to siblings, grandchildren, nieces, nephews, cousins and more.

Control of assets and how the money will be used (and when).

Used for over 7000 schools in the U.S. and abroad

No income restrictions-anybody can have an account

Wide variety of investment choices to choose from

Ease of use, automatic contributions enrollment, low entry dollar amount-most start at $100 initial and $25 each deposit after

Tax free and some states offer tax incentives if used for higher education

Gift 5 years worth of gifting to one 529 plan (60,000 single, 120,000 married)

Each state and or fund company has maximum aggregate contribution limit per beneficiary to a plan. You can go to: www.savingforcollege.com for more information

If used for higher education, 529 plans offer tax-free growth and tax-free withdrawals. They also allow for assigning a new beneficiary and allow final withdraw of money when no longer needed for higher education. You are taxed as ordinary income with a 10 percent penalty for this distribution or liquidation of the 529. Some advantages include the removal of money from your taxable estate and control over the age of redemption by the minor. Some states offer tax incentives, but beware-529 plans could interfere with loans and grants. Also, check very closely on fees and the ability to change investments inside the 529. You can convert an existing UGMA to a 529, but you need to sell all assets prior to this and incur capital gains/losses, then move the cash to the 529. Unlike starting a 529 plan in which you establish the age limit, the attained age for your state remains the same as the UGMA (Uniform Gifts to Minors Act) account after the transfer. You may want to start a separate 529 to control and/or eliminate the attained age restriction of a UGMA account. Always check with your tax adviser to see what the current gifting allowance is and if 529 plans are right for you.

For more information, visit www.savingsforcollege.com www.fastweb.com or www.findaid.com

You can establish a UGMA, set up gifting of $12,000 per year per individual donor, and place the funds in a brokerage or bank account for the benefit of the minor. Each state establishes at what attained age the minor may take over the assets.

TIP: You can purchase a term life insurance policy on yourself and on your spouse to cover the cost of education in the event of your death. Term is relatively inexpensive and you can specify 10-, 15-, 20-, or 30-year periods (**some companies are offering ROP-return of premium, at the end of the term and nothing has happened you get your premiums back or can opt for paid up insurance**). If your estate exceeds the federal estate tax credit you should place the policy in trust (irrevocable life insurance trust or ILIT) to keep it out of your taxable estate.

By completing steps 1, 2, and 3, you have identified items for your estate checklist, established your foundation for your wills/trusts, and organized your finances. These are items that you can take to your attorney, tax adviser, or financial adviser. You have also established records for your family.

Chapter IV

Step 4: How Much Life Insurance Do You Need?

The primary purpose for life insurance is the death benefit that it provides. Typically, you need to pass a physical to qualify for life insurance. The goal is to cover living expenses for your surviving spouse, pay for final expenses, and pay for any federal and state estate taxes due. Life insurance should not act as a retirement plan. The cost of insurance increases over time and can erode any cash value you may think that you are accumulating. If you do accumulate excess cash flow and start taking out annual withdrawals, and the policy lapses because of failure to make premium payments on the loans, you could face a tax bill on the investment gain you made. The formula would be the following:

Loans-Premiums Paid = Portfolio Gain × Your Tax Bracket

Make sure the life agent doesn't try to sell you a policy with distorted values for the projections of returns. The higher the return, the lower your premium will be. The problem is that if you run 10 percent or more and it does not perform, you could find yourself adding additional premiums in later years.

Basic types and purpose of life insurance

When you buy a life insurance policy, the face value of the policy is income tax free (not estate tax free) to your beneficiaries if the policy is held in your name, you have incidence of ownership,[13] or the estate is named as the beneficiary. However, it will be taxable at the face value of the estate; the interest is also taxable if not in an irrevocable life insurance trust for federal estate tax purposes. The ILIT is a separate trust that owns the life insurance policy for the benefit of the named beneficiaries. On death, the proceeds are income tax free and estate tax free. You cannot have any incidence of ownership, and you must send out the Crummey letters for the IRS to each named beneficiary, giving him or her the right to withdraw cash values. If anyone does withdraw cash, the withdrawal could void the trust. Further, any existing policies placed in an ILIT will carry a five-year look-back provision and must use the annual gifting provision allowed by the IRS, which is currently $12,000 per year per beneficiary.

- With *variable universal life (VUL)*, you have investment options to increase cash values to help offset premiums.

- *Universal life (UL)* is a variation of whole life; it allows you to adjust your premiums and death benefit up or down.

- *Whole life* combines a death benefit and accumulates cash value. The cash is a fixed amount of interest applied to your fixed premium for the life of the contract.

- *Second-to-die policies* are used primarily in trusts. Nothing happens when the first spouse dies, but on the second death, the insurance is collected. These policies are usually less expensive.

- *Term polices* have a fixed face value for a specified period of

---

13   Incidence of ownership means the power to change beneficiaries, borrow against cash values, surrender the policy, or pay premiums directly.

time: five, ten, fifteen, twenty, or thirty years. They are the least expensive and have no accumulation of cash. However, some companies offer a return of premium (ROP) at the end of the specified time. If you do not die you get your premiums back or can opt for paid up insurance.

- *Key-man or buy-sell agreements* are generally term insurance. You are buying insurance if you need to replace a key person or purchase another person's interest in the event of death.

You must have an insurable interest to obtain life insurance on another person.

4a) Life Insurance Calculator

Annual income needed for sur- $_____
viving spouse

Social security benefits $_____

Interest, dividends, pensions, $_____
other income

Total income (surviving spouse) $_____

Annual expenses $_____
(summarized to include mortgage, college costs, auto,
food, utilities, etc.; take this
from budget worksheet)

Credit card and other debt $_____

Final expenses (funeral costs) $_____

Total expenses $_____

Total expenses × life expec- $_____
tancy of surviving spouse

Total income minus expenses $_____

Liquid assets to pay off debt $_____
(stocks, bonds, mutual funds)

Life insurance on yourself $_____

Total liquid assets $_____

Shortfall $_____

You should evaluate your estate with an adviser to determine any federal or state death taxes that may be due, and add in the additional amount to cover those costs.

These are guidelines that depend on how much life insurance you can afford. To help determine the cost of life insurance (and long-term care insurance), go to www.lifehappens.org.

4b) Long-term Care Policies/Medicare/Medicaid

As we grow older (only around 35% of baby boomers have long term care policies), medical expenses and prescription medication generally increase. Several areas we will explore are long-term care policies, Medicare, and Medicaid programs. Long-term health care polices are designed to supplement health and living benefits as we get older. You have several choices: buy a long-term heath care policy, pay for nursing home or assisted living out of your pocket (note that each state has different costs for services—New Jersey can run $90,000 a year or more), or give away your assets and go on Medicaid. Long-term care polices provide a daily dollar rate for services needed. You can design your own benefit amount and any periods of waiting before the benefit goes into effect. So if you choose a 90-day waiting period, the first 90 days are out of your pocket, then your daily dollar amount starts paying for your care facility.

Things you should consider when researching a policy are as follows:

- Does the policy provide for in-home care, nursing home, or assisted living? The national average for nursing home care exceeds $54,000 per year. Assisted living is very expensive and generally requires large up-front fees to join with high monthly maintenance thereafter. Check all of this out prior to buying any policy-you need to make sure what you buy is going to cover what you get.

- What coverage such as prescription drugs, around-the-clock nursing care, and rent, is your premium quote covering? Is the coverage 100 percent or 80 percent?

- Does the policy contain a waiver of premium if you are confined to a nursing home or other care facility?

- What is the policy period for which you are being quoted? Is it three years, five years, ten years, or lifetime? If the policy is for a set number of years, you will run out of coverage at the end of the stated contract period. You then must pay for your care out of pocket.

- Is the policy portable? If you move to another state or facility, can you take the benefit with you?
- If you are younger and buy a long-term care policy, it may be beneficial to purchase a compounding benefit rate.
- Does it provide spousal discounts?
- Does it cover Alzheimer's, Parkinson's, or dementia?
- Check to see if your policy is tax deductible.
- Premiums are not guaranteed and may go up over time.
- Many corporations are now providing long-term care polices as a benefit.

Medicare and Medicaid

- Medicare (started in 1966) only covers nursing home care for a maximum of one hundred days, and only after an immediate hospital stay of four days. It does not provide for in-home nursing, or assisted living. It is a medical and drug prescription program sponsored by the government which goes into effect as primary medical coverage at age sixty-five. See www.medicare.gov.
- Medicaid is designed for transferring or selling your assets to pay for your nursing home care—not a good choice, but in some cases necessary. Beware of look-back provisions transferring assets (60 months for regular transfers (wills) and sixty months for trusts). After the look-back, Medicaid has no claim on the transferred assets. The IRS might have a claim if the assets were not filed under gift tax or not sold at 70 percent of fair market value. You can use IRS form 709 (gift tax) and use your 1 million exemption to transfer assets to avoid look-back provisions (you have currently

$12,000 per year per person to anybody, and 1 million life time-which can be used anytime for real estate, investments, art work, etc). Probate is one of the biggest collectors for Medicaid. For more information, go to Medicaid online at www.hcfa.gov or the following Web sites for more specific information on elderly care:

National Library of Medicine at

www.nlm.nih.gov/medline/nursinghomes.html

U.S. Department of Health at

www.medicare.gov/nhcompare/home.asp

Chapter V

Step 5: Keeping Track of Your Investments

You should make additional copies of the next page, and list all assets for each bank/broker account number, real estate, or any other asset of value. The IRS will require you to keep track of your cost basis on everything. When the sunset provision goes into effect in 2011, we will have a carryover for the capital gains tax. The current exemption will be $1.3 million, with additional spousal exemptions.

This formula should help you calculate cost basis:

The two methods of valuation are first in first out (FIFO) and last in first out (LIFO).

FIFO is the first share you bought and the first shares to be sold (stocks, bonds, mutual funds[14]). The problem is that the longer you hold the securities, the bigger your tax bill (capital gain) will be when you sell. It is necessary to keep track of your shares so that you can pick and choose which ones you want to sell—the chart on the next page will

---

14   Mutual fund cost basis is calculated two ways, lump sum or double category. Most mutual fund companies can explain the difference and which might be to your advantage to use.

assist you in keeping track of your investment cost basis. If you do not sell your shares before you die, your children will inherit the assets with a step-up in basis (no capital gains) unless you exceed the $1.3 million cost basis rollover set after 2011, in which case they would have to pay the difference over the exclusion amount.

Dividend reinvestment adds to your cost basis. To calculate this, multiply the per share dividend by the number of shares you owned when the dividend was issued, and add the total to your cost basis. Stock splits do not change the cost basis; instead, you receive additional shares. For example, 100 shares of stock at $30 per share gives you a cost basis of $3,000. If the stock then splits two for one, you will now have 200 shares with a value of $15 per share and a cost basis of $3,000.

If you need to calculate for stock splits or spinoffs or find the dividends paid, you can probably go to the company's Web site and find most of the information. Your broker or mutual-fund company can probably assist in this area as well.

Use the chart on the next page to help keep track of your investments.

Track your investment worksheet

Symbol Cusip	Date of purchase	# Shares	Purchase price	Market value	Date sold	Price sold	Gain/loss
Mutual funds							
___	___	___	___	___	___	___	___
___	___	___	___	___	___	___	___
___	___	___	___	___	___	___	___
___	___	___	___	___	___	___	___

Stocks

----- ---- ------ ------ ------ ---- ----- ------
----- ---- ------ ------ ------ ---- ----- ------
----- ---- ------ ------ ------ ---- ----- ------

Bonds

----- ---- ------ ------ ------ ---- ----- ------
----- ---- ------ ------ ------ ---- ----- ------

Stock
options

Option grant #	Date of grant/ expira- tion of option	# Options	Vesting dates	NSO/ ISO	Exer- cise date	Exer- cise price	# Shares sold	Profit
----	------	-----	------	-----	----	----	----	---

List each option separately

Personal Residence: Date of purchase _____ Purchase Price $_____

Currently there is a $500,000 exemption on capital gains on the sale of a primary residence every two years for couples filing joint; the exemption is $250,000 for single filers. Anything above the exclusion is subject to capital gains tax.

It's important to keep track of your cost basis. For nonqualified plans in 2011, the step-up in basis (fair market value at the time of death) is capped at $1.3 million per individual for capital gains tax. Anything over $1.3 million is now taxed at the current capital gains tax established by the IRS. Additional exemptions are allowed for married individuals. This is part of the trade-off for lower personal income tax with the Tax Reconciliation Act of 1997, which expires in 2011 if it is not repealed (known as the sunset provision for estate taxes). You will be required to prove your cost basis for all investments.

Chapter VI

Step 6: Asset Allocation Investment Cycle and Retirement Needs Analysis and Budget

As your life evolves, your investment strategies will change. The life cycle progresses as follows: when you are young and single, you don't put much thought into finances or estate planning. Then you attend college and get a job and become more concerned about your personal financial needs. When you get married and have children, everything changes. First you purchase housing, then college planning for your children. Then you think about investments, tax planning, retirement, estate planning, survivor protection, income protection, and finally succession-passing your assets on to your heirs and beneficiaries and not to the IRS.

In each phase of your life cycle, you need to assess where you are and where you are going. Every year, you should review where you are in terms of goals set. The life cycle progression may be considered in the following diagram:

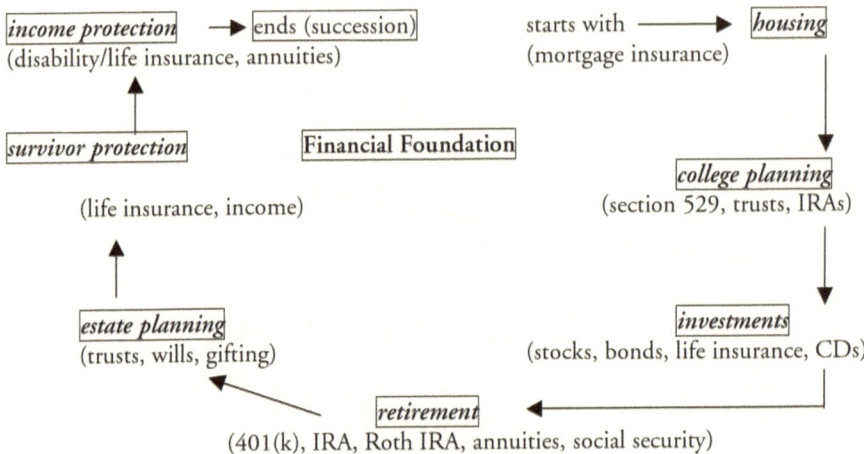

Most individuals do not save enough. In reality, the majority of people will rely on social security as the main source of retirement funding. A study by the Department of Human Services found the following for every one hundred people retiring at age sixty-five:

- Twenty-three will need to continue working—this is the reality for people who don't plan properly.

- Seventy-three will rely on others for support.

- Only four people will retire comfortably.

Bear in mind that, on average, a sixty-five-year old has a 50 percent chance of living to age ninety-two; so it is important not to overlook health care costs (including Medicare costs and coverage's) when planning for retirement (I have included a section on HSA plans for health care).

Now that you have completed your budget and know your net worth and net cash flow from income, you need to examine what expenses to cut and reallocate for retirement investments.

To apply for Social security benefits: www.socialsecurity.gov/apply-forbenefits or call 1-800-772-1213

6a) Retirement Budget

We have discussed your net cash flow while working; now let's examine your desired level of living following retirement. I remember in college my finance professor told us that we needed 65–75 percent of our working wages to live on in when we retire. I thought, "How can I retire on that amount of money when I can't live now on that? I want to retire and live a better lifestyle than when I am working!" To do so takes preparation, good investment strategies, and organization.

Most individuals think that once they retire, they no longer need to invest. This couldn't be farther from reality. For every dollar you take out, you will probably need to replace it with a minimum of $2. You need to be aware of withdrawal rates (see 4b below) and inflation and how they impact your money. For example, look at 3 percent inflation on $1 over the last thirty years. You need around $2.50 to equal that one dollar.

Expenses Needed for Retirement	Monthly	Annually
Mortgage	_____	_____
Property taxes	_____	_____
Auto(s)	_____	_____
Gas/maintenance/registrations	_____	_____
Utilities	_____	_____
Food	_____	_____
Telephone/cell phones	_____	_____
Cable	_____	_____
Credit cards	_____	_____

Insurance premiums/LTC[15]   _____   _____

Vacation home(s)   _____   _____

Travel/vacations planned   _____   _____

Medical premiums[16]   _____   _____

HSA account[17]

Taxes (quarterly estimates)[18]   _____   _____

All other expenses   _____   _____

Expenses total   _____   _____

Income

Pensions   _____   _____

Social security   _____   _____

Stocks/bonds/CDs   _____   _____

Annuities   _____   _____

IRAs   _____   _____

(You should roll over
401(k), 403(b)and other
qualified plans into your
IRA,

Rental property income   _____   _____

---

15   Life insurance and long-term health care insurance (LTC). See step 4b.

16   Go to www.medicare.gov and www.ssa.gov for social security and to www.irs.gov. These sites can provide calculators to help with cost estimates.

17   A health savings account is tax free for health care; you pay ordinary income for any other purpose. Go to www.opm.gov/hsa

18   The IRS requires a quarterly tax payment based on estimated passive income after retirement. Check with your accountant or tax adviser for more details.

All other income   _____   _____

Income total   _____   _____

Minus expenses   _____   _____

Total money available   _____   _____

6b) The Impact of Withdrawal Rates on Your Money

Withdrawal rate[19]	Years expected to last	Age incomes stops if you retire at 65
10%	11	76
9%	13	78
8%	15	80
7%	18	83
6%	21	86
5%	27	92
4%	33	98

Beneficiaries listed on your 401K, 403(b), and IRA's override your will.

We'll examine your risk tolerance (your financial DNA) in the next chapter. This withdrawal rate should make you go back and rethink your investment strategy. And remember, there is a 50 percent probability that you or your spouse will live to age ninety-two or longer.

The goal is to live off your assets-not on them

TIP: Go to www.opm.gov/hsa to look into the new health savings accounts (HSA), this is for alternative savings for health care retirement funds.

[?]   Based on historical data, utilizing a balanced portfolio of 50 percent stocks, 40 percent bonds, and 10 percent cash or equivalents and adjusted for inflation. These are only hypotheticals, and returns will vary based on your investment selection. This information is general and intended for educational purposes only.

Benefits of HSA accounts are many, it reduces your maximum out-of pocket liability, gives tax-deductions for most medical expenses and any portion you pay of your premiums, it is transferable if you change jobs, and you can use your tax-free contributions to pay for Medicare and other health care related items such as prescription drugs, co-pays, etc. If you are self-employed and a 1099 income earner, you must have a w-2 wage employee. The employer (LLC or C-Corp) and employees contributions are pre-tax dollars so you reduce FICA tax. The premiums are a tax deduction for the company and so are any contributions they make to an employees HSA account. The employees benefit with the same tax deductions of premiums and medical/prescription payments. If you are retired and have passive income you can have an HSA

Go to: www.opm.gov/hsa

Chapter VII

Step 7: Risk and Reward Questionnaire

The importance of finding your financial DNA (risk tolerance) has become more evident over the last few years of market and portfolio declines. Understanding what influences you to buy or sell can help you keep your investment strategy inline with your tolerance for actual losses. Although losing10 percent in your portfolio doesn't sound like a lot, consider that you need about 25 percent the following year to break even. When you fill out the questionnaire on the next page, be honest and don't cheat yourself.

What is your current allocation of investments?

Cash	_____%	Stock	_____%
Fixed income	_____%	Annuities	_____%
CDs	_____%	International	_____%
Real estate	_____%	Other	_____%

What is your involvement with the decision-making process of your investments?

_____

What is your experience with investments?
Stocks___ Bonds___ Mutual funds___
Options___ Annuities___ CDs_____ REITs[20]___

To find out where your risk and reward tolerances lie, assign each of the following questions a score. Numbering is as follows:

1. Strongly disagree
2. Slightly disagree
3. Neutral
4. Slightly agree
5. Strongly agree

_____ I am willing to accept greater price volatility in return for potentially higher long-term gains.

_____ Generating a return that offsets the effect of inflation is very important to me.

_____ I do not need current income from my investments.

_____ My investment goals are long term (greater than seven years).

_____ I am generally a risk taker.

_____

20   Real estate investment trust

_____   I am generally not a risk taker.

_____   I am willing to bear an above-average level of risk and can accept years of negative returns.

_____   I do not need to convert my investments into cash; I have enough liquid assets to meet my expenses.

_____   If I invested $10,000 in a long-term investment six months ago and its current value is now $8,500, I would probably keep the investment.

Total your score. The higher the number, the more risk you are willing to take.

Let's look at the following risk allocation categories.

- *Conservative*: Safety of principal is the main objective and minimal risk is involved.
- *Conservative to moderate*: The primary objective is safety of principal, but the secondary objective is growth of capital.
- *Moderate*: Growth of capital and safety of principal are both important. Moderate risk is acceptable to increase capital appreciation.
- *Moderate to aggressive*: The primary objective is growth of capital and a secondary goal is safety of principal. A fair amount of risk is acceptable to take advantage of greater growth opportunities.
- *Aggressive*: The primary objective is growth of capital. High risk is acceptable in seeking superior returns.

Generally, most people fall into a moderate investment attitude (a score of around a three to four in the above test). Balanced portfolios may be a better idea for these individuals. Have your financial adviser show you numbers that will better illustrate the asset allocation. You can find many modules for this, along with the ratings on most mutual funds, at Web sites such as www.morningstar.com or www.personal-fund.com.

For example, if your total score from the questions above is 17–22, you might consider a portfolio balance of 30 percent money market, 30 percent fixed income, and 40 percent equities. If your score is 29–34, you might consider 10 percent cash, 10 percent fixed income, and 80 percent equities. You need to match your goals to your investment risk, available investable income (from the budget worksheet), and time frame. Note: These examples are for educational purposes only and are not intended for investment advice. Check with your financial adviser or other financial professional for a more accurate measurement of your risk tolerances. In addition, always read a prospectus before investing.

Remember that all investments have some form or element of risk—CDs may not keep up with inflation, stocks may lose value, bonds can default, and so on. Common sense, organization, and research, and true diversification are your best protections for safeguarding your money and investments. Know what you are buying and the costs and risks associated with them.

If you are uncomfortable or don't understand what you are investing or getting into, *don't invest*. Remember the old saying: if it sounds too good to be true, it probably is. Always ask questions.

Chapter VIII

Step 8: Understanding Your Investments

The following information is intended to give you insight into how to assess, calculate, and analyze investments and risk tolerances.[21] We will discuss the history of the DOW; how to calculate returns, including how to calculate the internal dollar weighted rate of return for your mutual funds; limit and stop orders; and types of benchmarks money managers use. Understand what you are buying and the risk factors associated with it *before you buy or invest*. After all, it's your money.

---

21   Information is deemed to be accurate based on various research but is not guaranteed.

The History of the DOW, Types of Mutual Funds, Stocks, and Benchmarks

The fact remains that since 1926, the average return of corporate profits has run a pretty consistent 7.5 percent, and inflation has averaged around 3 percent–about 2.5 percent in the 1960s, 6.5 percent in the 1970s, 6 percent in the 1980s, 3 percent in the 1990s, and 2.5 percent since 2000.

Charles Dow formed the Dow Jones Industrial Average in 1884. He composed the top twelve or so stocks that he thought represented the economic strength of America. We have split the Dow into other major components such as the Transportation Index; the Standard & Poor's (S&P) 500; NASDAQ, which was founded in 1971 and consists mostly of technology stocks; the NASDAQ 100, known as the QQQ with the same ticker symbol, which tracks the top 100 companies of NASDAQ; the Russell 2000, which measures small-cap stocks (under 500 million in market capitalization); the Wilshire 5000, which is generally used to measure the total value of all U.S. stocks; and the Wilshire 4500, which measures small-and mid-cap companies. The government tracks consumer spending called the CPI, or consumer price index, for inflation. The CPI-U (U for urban) represents all consumer spending and accounts for over 80 percent of all households. Income tax brackets are adjusted to prevent consumers from paying higher taxes based on inflation. Core CPI is used for longer-term inflation trends and for tracking food and energy. CPI-W (wages) adjusts cost-of-living inflation and is primarily used to calculate social security increases, which was 4.1 percent for 2006.

You can find out more about the CPI on the Bureau of Labor Statistics Web site: www.bls.gov/cpi/home.htm and www.ssa.gov.

The Securities Investor Protection Act of 1970 (SIPC) is the equivalent of bank FDIC insurance. The general insurance coverage is for $500,000 per customer of the broker-dealer, $100,000 for cash and $400,000 for securities[22]. Government sponsorship is in the form of

---

22   Most brokerage houses have additional insurance per account.

board appointments made by the U.S. president, the Federal Reserve Board, and the U.S. Treasury. Most broker-dealers have additional insurance to cover larger losses.

8a) Basics to Know-Calculate Returns

To calculate your return on invested capital, price to earnings, and return on a mutual fund, use the following formula:

Current return on invested capital

Annual dividend $\underline{2.20}$ = 5% return

Current stock price44.375

Price to earnings (P/E)

Current stock price$\underline{44.375}$ = 10 times

EPS (earnings per share)   4.43   earnings

Return on mutual fund

$1 annual dividend

_____

$10 current offering price = 10% return

To see how you are really doing in comparison with the mutual fund published performance numbers, do the following:

1. Subtract your account balance at the start of the year from your current balance, divide the balance in half (including if it is negative), add back the money you had in the fund in the beginning of the year, and you have your average monthly balance.

2. From your current account balance, subtract both the amount you had in the fund at the start of the year and the additional investments. This gives you your total gain.

3. Divide your total gain or loss by your average monthly balance and multiply by 100. This gives you your dollar weighted total return for the year before taxes.

Finding your real rate of return can help you determine if the fund is worth keeping. Since 1986, the actual annualized return for mutual funds has been around 4 percent, compared with 11 percent + using the S&P 500 index with a buy-and-hold strategy. An excellent Web page to help determine the return and cost is www.personalfund.com. Always keep track of your original price and the number of shares you purchase.

8b) Market, Limit, and Stop Orders

When you buy or sell a stock, it is referred to as T+3 (trade plus three days to settle). This means that you have that amount of time to pay money due or collect money from the sale.

When companies pay dividends, generally on a quarterly basis, you can take the cash or reinvest the dividend into the company stock. When you reinvest the dividends into the stock, you raise your cost basis and generally end up with odd lot or fractional shares of stock, which are difficult to sell. The board sets the record date on which you are entitled to receive the dividend; however, you must be a stockholder of record prior to that record date. The ex-dividend date (to be eligible for the dividend) is generally two business days before the record date.

You buy auto insurance, homeowner's insurance, and life insurance to protect your homes, cars, and liabilities. So why not buy profit-and-loss protection with the use of limit orders, stop-loss orders, and so on? Here is how they work.

Market Orders

A *market order* is an order to buy or sell a stock immediately at the best execution price.

Limit Orders

A *limit order* is an order to buy or sell a security at a specified price or better for a specified time.

A *buy limit* is the maximum price a buyer is willing to pay. If you want to buy a stock for $50 per share and the current price is $55 per share, you should put in a 50GTC (good 'til cancelled) order. The stock will be executed if it hits $50 or below.

A *sell limit* is the minimum price a seller is willing to take for his or her security. If you bought a stock for $40 and the minimum amount you will take is $65, you would enter a sell limit order of 65GTC. The stock will not sell unless it hits at least $65 per share.

Stop Orders

Buy stop orders take advantage of increasing stock prices. If you bought the stock at $25 per share and think it will go to $35 per share, you would place a buy stop order at $35. If it hits $35, the order becomes a market buy order, the trade will be executed at the next trade price, and you will lock in your profit. If it never hits the target price, it will expire.

Sell stop orders are used to stop a stock price from declining too low. Let's say you put in a sell stop at $50 and the current price is $65. If the price goes below $50, it will trigger the sell order and convert it to a market order. The stock will sell at next price available, and you limit your losses.

Stop limit orders help protect profit. If you bought a stock at $60 and it's currently at $75, which gives you a paper profit of $15 per share (it isn't a profit until you sell and put the money in your pocket), you put in a stop limit order. If the stock starts to decline and hits the stop price, it activates the trade. The sell stop limit says that if you put in $70 for the stop limit, you will get the next trade at $70 or above.

When the stockbroker pulls up his or her screen for equity trading and the broker places an execution order, the computer asks if it is a market order (immediate trade at market price), limit order, stop order, or stop and limit order. The price gets recorded and execution will take place at one end or the other, taking profit or protecting losses.

Other types of risks to consider when deciding to purchase a security are as follows:

- Credit: the borrower's inability to repay the loan or debt
- Interest rate: the value of the bond will decline due to rising interest rates
- Inflation: the value of the asset will decline and will not keep up with inflation (bond interest); thus, your buying power is decreased
- Liquidity: the ability to sell the security
- Political climate: influences of government policies (both domestic and foreign) that affect values

Selling short is selling a security you do not own. Instead, you are borrowing from the broker, who in turn borrows from inventory, other margin customers, or other institutions that lend securities. You sell, or borrow, at the current market price and hope that the stock falls in price. You then buy the stock at the lower price, replace the borrowed stock to the broker, and profit from the difference. All short selling must be from a margin account. For example, if the shares sold short at $80 and the market drops to $60, the profit is $20 per share. The same could happen on the loss end of the deal: a stock bought at $80 goes to $100, leaving you with a loss of $20 per share.

Selling short against the box is when the investor actually owns the stock and wants to sell but not deliver the shares yet. He or she may pledge or use the stock to secure a loan and then later deliver the long shares to pay back the broker. This also defers any tax consequences of the sale.

Program trading, which is becoming a large part of the volatility of Wall Street, is when institutional investors use computerized programs to trigger buy or sell orders. This can create large blocks of stocks in the market. If nobody buys, the price keeps dropping until it hits the desired target price of another investor. The same old rule applies: for every buyer there must be a seller, and for every seller there must be a buyer.

The *OTC (over-the-counter) marketplace* is a negotiated marketplace between broker-dealers. The orders do not go through an exchange, but instead are completed via the telephone. Each broker-dealer firm has its own traders to handle the transactions. Most broker-dealers will not allow stop or limit orders on OTC securities because there is no specialist to handle or watch the price.[23] The pink sheets quote trades in the OTC market not traded on the NASDAQ. The NASDAQ trades more active OTC stocks. Other sources are newspapers.

The *Instinet market* is when institutions trade between one another. Mutual fund companies, pensions, banks, and insurance companies provide one another with quotes on securities that they want to buy or sell.

---

23   Specialists hold a seat on the exchange and agree to maintain an orderly market in securities. They buy when others are selling, and they sell when others are buying. They buy and sell in their own account and act as agent for others. They must qualify with the board of exchange and have enough capital to maintain large positions in each security in which they specialize. Specialists handle most of the orders, from various brokers on the trading floor that cannot be executed immediately by the broker—stop orders, limit orders, and so on.

Managers style their investment and performance objectives by specific benchmarks and compete against an unmanaged index. Fund managers try to beat the benchmarks. For example, let's say the S&P 500 unmanaged index was down 18 percent, but the fund manager was only down 10 percent. The fund manager used the S&P 500 for his benchmark, but his performance was much better. He still lost your 10 percent.

My personal benchmark is zero with absolute returns vs. relative returns (comparing benchmarks). Diversification of your assets and asset classes and avoiding overlap (options, ETF's, bonds, value, growth, REIT's, etc) can help reduce volatility and enhance returns

8c) The Primary Benchmarks

- *Wilshire 5000* tracks the entire stock market of over 6,000 U.S. stocks.

- *Wilshire 4500* tracks the performance of small-and mid-cap stocks of the Wilshire 5000 but not of the S&P 500.

- *Russell 3000* tracks three thousand companies with the highest market capitalization (or market value based on the number of outstanding shares × the stock price). These companies represent over 90 percent of the total value of U.S. companies.

- *Russell 2000* consists of the smallest two thousand companies in the Russell 3000 index.

- *Russell 1000* is one thousand of the most valuable companies of the Russell 3000 companies in leading industries and market caps exceeding $9 billion.

- *S&P 400* tracks four hundred midsize companies with market caps up to $3 billion.

- *S&P 500* covers a basket of five hundred widely held stocks. It is weighted by market value and is used most often to gauge the overall U. S. market performance.

- *S&P 600* covers small-cap companies valued between $250 and $900 million.

- *NASDAQ 100* tracks the top one hundred tech blue chips.

- *Lehman Brothers Aggregate Bond Index* covers government, investment-grade, corporate, and asset-backed bonds with maturities of short and long durations.

- *MSCI EAFE* is the Morgan Stanley Capital International market weighted average of nine hundred-plus securities from Europe, Australia, and the Far East.

- *MSCI EM* is the emerging market index/benchmark.

- *U.S. treasury bills* are based on the average monthly yield of 30-day treasury bills.
- *NAREIT Equity REIT Index* tracks equity REITs.

Everybody thought the markets would keep going up. But guess what? They didn't. Don't make the same mistake twice. Harvest your profits and reinvest them somewhere safe.

Chapter IX

Step 9: Mutual Fund Checklist: Items You Need to Address Before Investing

In this chapter we will look at what type of investor you are; the options for paying commissions—fee based or a combination of fee based and commission; and a checklist for what you should look for before buying mutual funds and other investments.

9a) A Little Housekeeping to Understand Your Options for Fees Charged

Before we begin, what type of investor are you? Growth or value? Fundamental? Technical?

- *Value investors* generally focus on buying stocks that appear to be bargains relative to the company's net worth and low P/E ratios. Some circumstances that may make a stock a value buy include: companies that are trading below intrinsic value because of recent competition or management changes, or an industry that is currently out of favor with investors.

- *Growth investors* like companies that are growing quickly, newer companies, and emerging industries. They have greater potential for quick stock appreciation, higher earnings per share (EPS), and, of course, higher risk.

- *Contrarian investors* are value investors to the limit. They believe the time to buy is when no one else wants to, or they focus on stocks or industries that are temporarily out of favor.

There are two basic types of investment research: fundamental and technical.

- *Fundamental investors* analyze data about the company and operations. Fundamental analysts evaluate figures and try to assess the company's prospects and determine what the shares may be worth after evaluating the company's potential. Buy-and-hold investors generally focus on fundamental data.

- *Technical investors* focus on the company's stock price rather than its operations. They prefer to identify trading patterns on charts that reflect price history and trading volume for a particular stock. The technical analyst helps them identify stocks that are trending higher or lower and trends in the market as a whole.

A combination of fundamental and technical analysis, along with diversification of growth and value, can give you a balance in your investment portfolios.

Independent asset management (IAM) accounts, sometimes referred to as WRAP fee programs, are flat-percentage-rate accounts at brokerage firms. You pay a flat fee ranging from 1–3 percent (whatever you negotiate) for mutual funds, stocks, and bonds. The advantage is that the flat fee is all you pay. You buy mutual funds at net asset value (NAV), which are Class A shares without the sales load, and pay no commissions on stock trades. There is usually a cap on how many trades per year you're allowed to avoid day traders and no or low markup on bonds, which produces higher yields. It can be a real advantage for mutual funds to avoid all the hidden costs (except 12b-1 fees that companies charge for advertising) that could raise the total cost of ownership above 3 percent. Commissions on stocks in and out (buy and sell) can be costly and can directly affect your profit.

If you prefer to pay commission for each trade, try to keep the commission to 2 percent or less for your stock trades—and compare bond quotes and charges for front-end load mutual funds. You need to look at overall costs in mutual funds. I prefer a flat-fee program because you control your cost, eliminate commissions on security trades, and generally deduct the fee when filing taxes. It also takes the "trading" or "churning" out of the picture. I have always thought that the turnover by brokers for commissions in investments benefited them more than it did the client-no trades, no commissions, no payday!

The fee is something you never see in mutual funds because it's taken out of fund performance, and bonds already contain a mark-up. With managed money or WRAP account programs, you see the fee up front every quarter-even though it is generally less than that of traditional funds (you buy mutual funds at NAV, bonds with little or no mark-up, and no commissions on stock trades). You need to get over the psychological barrier of the fee dilemma; plus, it is an advisory fee, so it is generally tax deductible, which brings down your cost.

If you allow discretionary trading (giving someone else the authority to trade on your behalf without asking you), make sure you do a complete background check. See if the person is registered with the NASD, see www.nasd.com, and SEC, see www.sec.gov. If trading futures, make sure the person is registered with the Commodity Futures Trading Commission. Go to www.nfa.futures.org or www.cftc.gov or call 1-800-621-3570.

9b) The Mutual Fund (and Other Investments) Checklist

- Does it meet your investment objectives and risk profile?
- What are the risks with this fund or investment?
- What is the liquidity (how easy can you sell this investment and at what cost)?
- What is the overlap (same stocks or bonds held) of top holdings in each of the funds you pick?
- What is the investment objective of the fund?
- Is the portfolio manager turnover high? How long have the current managers managed the fund?
- What is the portfolio turnover ratio? The higher the turnover (trading), the higher the cost, because you pay for commissions on trades inside the fund.
- Keep track of what you paid for the investment, not the advertised yields or stated returns. You can then see what you would get back if you sell it later. See step 8a.
- Pay attention to current returns—not just the one-, three-, five-, or ten-year returns, as they can be deceiving. You could put in $10,000 during a bad year or midyear and lose

money, but the fund will show a positive return for each of the periods. *You need a blend of equity and bonds, cash, and alternative investments to stay ahead of the game.*

- Ask for current; three-month and one-, two-, and three-year performance numbers and after-tax return numbers. A good Web page for looking at fund performance and costs (it's unaudited) is www.sec.gov/cgi-bin/srch-edgar.

- Remember, past performance is no guarantee of future results or performance.

- If the fund is underperforming in comparison with other similar funds, then sell and move your money to a better fund. Check out the Web site www.personalfund.com for comparisons to other funds, expense ratios, and returns as well as costs to own the fund and trading costs.

- Does the broker/bank, mutual fund company, or annuity company offer investment policies?[23]

- Consider cost of ownership, which includes redemption fees, turnover (how often the money managers trade stocks/bonds), commissions, taxes, 12b-1 fees, manager fees, and distribution fees (higher fees mean lower returns). Read the prospectus.

- Consider sales commissions (front-end loads are charges you pay up front, which reduce your investment by that amount). Don't confuse load/no-load with fund fees, commissions on trading costs, 12b-1 fees, and manager fees.

- Does the fund offer break points on purchases? Make sure you keep track. Don't let a broker put you into multiple funds to avoid giving you break points, as it affects his com-

23   Investment policies provide protection for all. They specify your risk tolerance, type of investments, investment style (conservative, moderate, and so on), and objectives. The policy puts everything in writing and should be reviewed periodically as your life events change.

mission. You can also sign a letter of intent (LOI) that states your intention to make your investment total the break-point level over the next thirteen months. If you do not meet the break-point level, you may have to pay back the difference. You can also backdate a LOI for ninety calendar days.

- Class B shares are no-load and up front, but they have declining sales charges (CDSC) over a specified period of time—know what they are, how much, and how long. You also incur 12b-1 fees. After the CDSC charges are gone, they convert to class A shares.

- Consider annual charges, which are fees generally charged for smaller accounts and IRAs. Fees vary.

Expense ratios are what the internal fund charges for managers and 12b-1 fees (the funds charged for advertisement). Pay attention to turnover in a mutual fund: the higher the turnover (buying and selling), the more it adds to the cost of ownership. You, the investor, pay commissions every time a trade is made, and the commission trades are not listed in the management or fund costs. You need to dig deep in the prospectus to find them. A great Web page that includes the total cost of ownership, including turnover costs, is www.personalfund.com. It has several options for pricing. If you invest mainly in mutual funds, it's worth the approximate $200 annual subscription. It also gives you comparable funds with lower costs. You can also visit www.sec.gov/cgi-bin/srch-edgar (Securities and Exchange Commission) for unaudited mutual fund, annuity, and company reports and other useful information.

- Ask for after-tax returns. Mutual fund companies now must report them.

- First rule of thumb: take your highest point of growth and put a stop-loss or limit order (see step 8) in place to protect your profit or limit your loss. For example, if you have $100,000 and it grows to $115,000, from $115,000 you might place a stop order at a loss of 10 percent from the high, or-$11,500, which still leaves you a profit of $3,500. Each individual investor can establish his or her own percentage of comfort. You can do the same with individual money managers, and with individual stocks with limit and stop-loss orders, which are discussed later.

- Second rule of thumb: you need to take the emotion out of investing; it is about buying low and selling high and making a *profit*. Let's get real here. If you sell a stock, bond, mutual fund, or any other security, don't act like somebody cut off your arm! If you bought the stock at $25 per share and sold for $40 per share in the same year, and your tax bracket was 30 percent, you made $40-$25 = $15 per share profit. Multiply by 30 percent for your capital gains tax of $4.50 per share, and you have $10.50 per share net profit! That's a 70 percent profit and 85 percent profit if you hold it one year or longer!

- Ask the brokerage firm, bank, or mutual fund company whether it offers investment policies. Investment policies are the terms and conditions of your investment risk tolerance and comfort level. They spell out whether you are a conservative or moderate investor and help protect you from anybody going outside your comfort zone. You need to understand more about the downsides of arbitration and mediation contracts that you sign with brokerage houses. Always keep track of your original purchase price (step 5) and your original confirmation tickets from the brokerage or fund company when you buy or sell any security.

Understanding the previous checklist and benchmarks as well as the following pages, can help you make the right selections in mutual funds, ETFs, managed money, bonds, REITs, hedge funds, commodities, options, and fee structure.

Chapter X

Do It Right: Learn Before You Invest

Mutual funds provide an economical way for investors of moderate (and not so moderate) means to obtain the same professional advice and diversification of investments as wealthy individuals. All shareholders share in the dividends, income, and capital gains (less expenses and fees) of the funds in which they invest. Generally, using advisers benefits the investor because financial advisers have the tools to reduce the number of funds selected, help eliminate any overlap, and narrow the type of funds to stay within your risk profile (since there are over 15,000 mutual funds) based on your individual criteria. However, it is you who ultimately must decide what funds best fit your needs for short-term, intermediate, and long-term goals and retirement investments. That is what this book aims to do: help you obtain the correct information, understand what you are investing in, and how to keep what you make.

Who Regulates Mutual Funds?

The Securities Exchange Commission (SEC) regulates mutual funds under the Investment Act of 1940, the Securities Act of 1933, and the Securities Exchange Act of 1934. These laws state that mutual funds must be sold with a prospectus that outlines commissions and explains fees, investment objectives, and expenses. I strongly recommend reading the prospectus or having someone explain it to you. There is no easy method for understanding the complexities of mutual funds. Most managers never disclose what overlap exists, what is good for taxable or non-taxable accounts, or what is the internal rate of return to the investor. You can request what the after-tax returns are; managers are required to disclose this, and you can calculate the internal rate using the formula in step 8a. Always look at the holdings inside the funds you own to help avoid overlap and add to true diversification.

The operation of a mutual fund consists of a board of directors/trustees, officers, attorneys, an independent public accountant, custodian, administrator, transfer agent, principal underwriter, investment adviser—and you, the shareholder.

Almost all funds are all externally managed; they generally have no employees and hire outside investment managers, broker-dealers, and banks.

Most funds are open-ended, which means that they pay capital gains or losses at the end of each year and continually issue new shares that can be purchased or redeemed at any time-like a stock for current end-of-day value or NAV. The value is the closing price for each trading day; it is derived by taking its total value, subtracting expenses, and dividing by the total number of shares outstanding.

A closed-end fund may issue stocks or bonds and trades on an exchange or purchased from a broker. The share price is negotiated at the end of each day, based on supply and demand or market conditions. You buy or sell and receive market price at the time of the sale.

Investor note: Most companies no longer offer pension plans, so it is up to you to save for your retirement. Most of your contributions, if you participate, will be to your 401(k), IRA, or other qualified plans that your employer offers. I find it imperative to invest in not only your retirement plan but also individual investments and to understand your investment options and watch your investments. Look for nice, steady, incremental growth each year. Rebalance your portfolios. Typically, I rebalance cash—I take profit (monthly through dividends or interest) and reinvest it.

Many mutual fund companies now offer balanced portfolios with a choice of the asset allocation classes all in one account such as large-cap value, small/mid-cap, growth, income, bonds, and various styles like aggressive, moderate, conservative, etc. The advantages of this plan generally include the daily rebalancing and reallocating of funds or cash in your portfolio. This takes the guesswork out of what and when to buy or sell, which could be advantageous for the less-experienced investor-and, in many cases, the experienced investor as well.

By law, mutual funds must pass on income and capital gains from investments to the shareholders in both qualified and nonqualified plans. In nonqualified mutual funds, if you sell before one year, the sale is considered a short-term capital gain and is taxed at your current income tax rate. Selling after one year or longer is a long-term capital gain, currently at 15 percent of your profit. The new NAV, after the fund has declared its end-of-year capital gain distribution, is decreased by that capital gains distribution. In other words, if you pay $20 per share and the capital gain is $5, your new value, or NAV, is $15. You buy more shares at the new NAV and hope for appreciation in the coming year. Your other option is to take the capital gain as a cash distribution and reinvest it in other funds. If your current mutual funds are performing well, why sell? By doing this, you are, in essence, rebalancing your portfolio.

If you have closed-end funds, you are issued a 1099B form. In a closed-end fund, the fund pays tax on the gains at the corporate tax rate and reinvests the proceeds back into the fund versus distributing the long-term gains to the shareholders. If this occurs, you must file a separate Form 2439, Notice to Shareholders of Long-Term Capital Gains. You report this on line 64, page 2, of your 1040. Your cost basis is increased by the difference between long-term capital gains not distributed and the taxes paid by the fund.

Always check the top holdings inside the fund. You want to avoid overlap (the same stocks) by choosing different funds and strategies to diversify.

"Rebalancing" and "asset allocation" have been buzzwords for the last few years. In reality, rebalancing quarterly, semiannually, and annually have not been as successful as actively rebalancing daily or monthly and reallocating profits to other areas for further diversification.

The example below assumes you started with a $10,000 investment and watch it over a five-year period:[24]

Rebalanced quarterly:	$9,609
No rebalancing:	$9,900
Benchmark S&P 500, LBAB (Lehman bond index)	$11,090
Rebalanced actively (daily or monthly)	$12,020

Dollar-cost averaging uses the strategy of investing a fixed dollar amount at regular intervals—every two weeks, monthly, or quarterly. This takes advantage of market fluctuations over time and reduces the average share price you pay.

TIP: If you want additional rebalancing, instead of re-investing dividends back into stock or mutual funds, take the cash and invest in something else or spend it. If you have high yield or income funds, you also might want to take the cash and invest somewhere else for further diversification. One of the problems I find with re-investing stock dividends is that you end up with a lot of odd lot or fractional shares that are hard to get rid of; the advantage to re-investing stock dividends is that it increases your cost basis for a future sale.

Best bet-find actively managed funds or money managers that rebalance daily.

10a) The Basics: Classification of Funds

Understand the difference:

Load funds charge up-front sales commissions, usually a class A share. This can be as high as 8.75 percent, plus your management fees, trading costs, distribution fees, redemption fees, taxes, etc. Class A shares generally offer lower fund fees versus C shares or B shares.

No-load funds have no up-front sales commissions, but they still have trading costs, manager's fees, 12b-1 fees, distribution costs, redemption costs, and taxes.

Class A shares generally have the lowest expense ratios, but you pay an up-front fee ranging from around 3.5–8.75 percent. No charges are incurred to sell the fund.

Class B shares are no-load up front (no sales commission), but they have CDSC on the back end if you sell them. The charges can range as high as 6 percent and decline each year, up to six years. Plus you have 12b-1 fees, which are .25 percent. At the end of the CDSC, the B shares convert to A shares.

Class C shares are no-load and generally have higher administrative charges. They carry a one-year CDSC charge of 1 percent if sold before one year is up.

Institutional funds include class D and I. They are typically sold in defined contribution plans and brokerage WRAP account programs, in which a flat fee is charged for the mutual funds.

The following pages will discuss types of funds, the history of the Dow, benchmarks, and other items to help educate you about how things work, how managers make decisions on investments, and what factors (such as the CPI) affect or influence outcomes of investments. We will also go over various types of investments and comparisons.

10b) Types of Funds We See Most Often

Most funds are benchmarked against an unmanaged index-a passive index like the S&P 500. Here are some examples of common funds:

- *Large-cap growth funds* generally invest in companies with long-term earnings that are consistent and expect to grow

---

24   Source: Based on a Thompson Financial report using a $10,000 investment at NAV on 12/31/99 through 12/31/2004 and no withdrawals.

significantly over time. They generally pay no or low dividends. The unmanaged index is the S&P 500.

- *Large-cap value funds* look for long-term growth from companies that are considered undervalued compared with an unmanaged stock index (passive). They generally have a below-average price-to-earnings (P/E) ratio. Normally these funds have an average price-to-earnings ratio, are benchmarked with the S&P Mid-Cap 400 Index, and pay higher dividends.

- *Mid-cap growth funds* generally have an above-average price-to-earnings ratio and are expected to grow faster than an unmanaged stock index. The Lipper Mid-Cap Growth Index is the unmanaged benchmark.

- *Small-and mid-cap value funds* are generally construed as undervalued, have a lower P/E ratio, and seek long-term moderate growth. The Russell 2500 Value Index is the unmanaged benchmark.

- *Small-cap growth funds* are weighted against the S&P Small Cap 600 Index, generally have above-average P/E ratios, and are expected to grow considerably faster than an unmanaged stock index. They also can be very volatile.

- *S&P 500 Index A* is a passively managed index that benchmarks the performance of the S&P 500 on a reinvested basis. The stocks will rise and fall with the market, so volatility becomes an issue.

- *Life cycle funds* are fairly new. They invest more aggressively when you are younger, and as you get older, they start to invest more conservatively and eventually invest for income.

- *Balanced funds* generally have a mix of growth and dividend paying value stocks and higher-quality bonds. Balanced funds provide a more stable (less volatile) portfolio;

the bonds help balance out and support income and reduce volatility. The S&P 500 Index is the general benchmark.

- *International value funds* generally invest in large capitalized corporations with a record of stable earnings and consistent dividend payments.

- *Emerging market funds* target securities with very high return potential and carry very high volatility. They deal with countries that are in an emerging growth stage of development. Generally, they are pure growth, and risk occurs if they don't develop, have unstable governments, and so on. They are benchmarked with the Lipper Small-Cap Growth Funds and the Russell 2000 Growth Index.

- *Developing market funds* seek long-term, worldwide growth from companies that will benefit from current economic themes and new technology. They usually have established, stable governments and great potential to develop trade with other countries, but they can be risky and volatile. They are weighted against the MSCI (Morgan Stanley Emerging Market Index).

- *Income funds* try to provide a steady stream of income from fixed investments and higher-paying stock dividends. The target is around 6 percent. The Lipper Income Fund Index is the unmanaged benchmark.

- *Bond funds* invest in various investment-grade corporate bonds as well as government bonds. They are used primarily to help diversify portfolios outside the equities market, with expected average yields of around 5–6 percent. The primary index is the Lipper Intermediate Investment Grade Debt Funds Index.

- *Growth and income funds* generally balance between stocks and bonds and try for a return of 7 percent or greater. The Lipper Income Funds Index is the unmanaged benchmark.

- *Floating rate funds* seek low volatility with high returns. They invest in senior-secured floating-rate loans made to U.S. corporations by larger domestic banks and are designed to keep up with current interest rates. They generally have a shorter duration (time frame to maturity) of three to five years. The Lipper Loan Participation Fund Index is the passive unmanaged benchmark.

- *Municipal bond funds* invest in higher-grade municipalities to generate federal tax-free income. Most states will exempt state interest if you live in the state in which you purchase the bonds. Beware of the alternative minimum tax (AMT) inside the bond funds-AMT can run 25 percent or more. The Lipper High Yield Muni Debt Fund Index is the unmanaged benchmark.

- *High-yield bond funds* offer higher returns and are issued by companies with poor credit ratings or poor credit histories. They are issued to raise capital (debt offerings versus issuing new stock) and pay higher yields than investment-grade securities. The risk is default. Benchmarks are the Lipper High Current Yield Fund and the S&P 500 Index.

10c) Specialty Funds, Alternative Investments (Hedge Funds, Options, REITs, Index Funds, ETFs, Money Managers, Reverse mortgages, Interest only, ARM's, and Traditional Fixed Rate Mortgages)

Let's look at some specialty funds and strategies: options, commodities, REITs, fund of funds, and hedge funds. These funds are referred to as alternatives, typically used to offset standard investments, and are generally noncorrelated[24] to the market. They usually help reduce risk and increase overall performance. In addition, an indepth discussion on mortgages.

• *Fund of funds* are mutual funds investing in a basket of other mutual funds. They have a management team overseeing, rebalancing, reallocating, and handling due diligence (making sure the funds meet and maintain the requirements, objectives, and performance) of the basket of funds in the portfolios. Some hedge funds use this strategy as well. The investment management company Horizon Investments uses a different strategy and asset reallocation called "dynamic asset allocation and rebalancing." This is an active strategy that varies the portfolio composition in response to changing market conditions and expectations. Asset classes with the most profit potential are given more weight than weaker asset classes. This is similar to static asset allocation in its use of diversification to reduce volatility, but it differs in its ability to reallocate funds to the current market leadership and away from market laggards. For more information, go to www.horizoninvestments.com.

TIP: Make sure you understand the various layers of fees involved with fund of funds before you invest. Take the time to evaluate the fees versus performance.

• *Hedge funds* number around eight thousand; some are SEC[25]-registered and some are not. Hedge funds come under the Investment Company Act of 1940 and invest in various, generally noncorrelated, securities to the market. Most managers have a vested interest in the portfolios, since they themselves have a great deal of money invested in their own hedge funds. They are paid on performance and use a targeted-return approach. Some of the strategies used include investing in currencies, short sales of securities, leveraged (borrowed) money, futures, options on futures, index options, and arbitrages. Hedge funds generally are used to offset the markets, enhance performance, and

---

24   "Noncorrelated to the market" are investments that capitalize on the opposite direction such as options, derivatives, real estate, arbitrages, short selling, etc. In some cases they do better when the market is volatile or declining.

reduce risk. Some are "fund of funds," which use the strategies of many managers who oversee the portfolios, allowing for many different strategies in one account. In recent years, the minimum dollar required investment amounts have been reduced to as low as $50,000 and $100,000 for accredited investors.[26] Compensation (manager's fees) and bonuses based on performance over the targeted (hurdle) return are fund costs. If the targeted return is 7 percent and the fund does 10 percent, the managers are paid anywhere from 10–20 percent of the money over the targeted hurdle, not on the entire portfolio. Many pensions and wealthy individuals have used hedge funds to have a noncorrelated investment to the stock market. In some cases, managed portfolios have incorporated a "hedge fund to fund" and "commodity fund" inside the standard asset classes of large-cap value, growth, small/mid-cap, international, and bond ETFs or managed bond portfolios—all in one account.

Managed commodity funds (mutual funds) invest in raw materials such as wheat, corn, aluminum, copper, gas, and oil. These can be hedges against inflation; commodity prices tend to go up with inflation, while stock prices do better in declining inflation. Mutual funds are not allowed to buy commodities; they buy a derivative instrument, which is a contract whose value is based on the performance of an underlying investment, like a futures contract. These are noncorrelated assets to the market. Managed commodities funds can potentially help reduce risk and enhance overall performance.

- *Managed options and option writing* are what I refer to as "the other income." Very few people understand option trading. The Options Clearing Corporation (OCC) issues all options that are listed on the Chicago Board of Options Exchange (CBOE). If you're buying or selling, the standard option contract is for 100 shares or one option contract.

25   Securities and Exchange Commission

All options expire at 3:30 PM Central Standard Time on the third Friday of the expiry month. All options (short-term profit or loss) are reported on Schedule D. You can offset short-term losses against long-term gains. In very general terms, if you own a stock and want to sell an option, you, as the owner of the stock, write or sell a "call option" if you think the stock is going to go up in value, or you sell a "put option" if you think the stock will decline. Owning the stock is considered covered-call writing; if the stock is called away, you get the premium for the call or put plus the difference of the strike price, which is the agreed price to buy or sell the security at a predetermined date.

Here is an example of an investor buying a put option (you think the stock is going lower, and you do not want to own the stock):

Joe Investor buys a put option (he thinks the stock is going to go lower) on XYZ Company for a premium of $300. The underlying stock is at $40, which is the agreed strike price. If the stock drops to $30 per share on the open market, and the investor exercises the option and buys the stock at $30 and sells back to the writer of the put for $40, the profit would be $1,000 minus the $300 premium, or a net of $700. If the stock increases or stays the same, the investor would lose the $300 premium paid and the writer (owner of the stock) would keep the $300 premium.

This example is for buying a call option because you think the stock is going up and you do not want to own the stock:

---

26   Accredited investors are generally individuals with a net worth of $1-1.5 million.

Joe Investor buys a call option on XYZ Company for $400 to buy 100 shares at $50 per share. The price goes to $70 during the option contract, the investor exercises the option to buy the stock at the agreed strike price of $50 per share and sells the stock on the open market for $70 per share; making $2,000 profit minus the $400 premium paid. If the stock does not increase or stays the same, the loss risk is limited to the $400 premium paid.

People buy or sell calls and puts to create income. You can do both, buy a put and call option on the same stock. It's like buying insurance; it lowers your overall profit because you can't win on both ends. The more "in the money" you are, the more likely the stock will get called away. "In the money" is if you sell a call at $1.50 per contract (one option contract is 100 shares of stock) for example, and the strike price is $25. Let's say the stock goes to $25.50 or above. The investor or buyer of the option will probably call the stock away and sell it at a later date on the open market to make money. You keep the premium and the difference to the strike price of the stock. If the stock price drops, the call will expire worthless, and you keep the premium and the stock.

If you were the owner or writer of the stock, you hope nothing happens and you keep the stock and the premium paid. You wrote the options to increase your income and diversify your portfolio. If you are the buyer of the call or put, you are hoping you can buy the stock at the agreed prices and sell to make a profit.

Short selling is a little more dangerous, because you are borrowing the stock from the broker and promising to repay with the same stock at a future date. There are many types of options, puts, calls, straddles, leaps, index options, covered calls, covered puts, naked options, and combinations.

I find that when you utilize companies that specialize in options trading through individual funds or managed portfolios, you fare better than trying to guess the market as an individual. A great way to practice is to go to www.bigcharts.com and look under the Options tab, or go directly to the American Stock Exchange at www.amex.com. Covered-call writing is extremely useful for individuals who have a highly concentrated stock position with a low cost basis-you have a lot of stock you bought cheap and do not want to sell for capital gains and dividends, or it is restricted stock under rule 144. Companies will put your stock in a portfolio and write calls/puts, generate additional income, and protect the stock with the use of a margin account (borrowed money). This is used to protect the stock with cash to pay for the call versus selling the stock.

> If using options, you need to separate portfolio performance with income performance; otherwise, put your money in a total return investment. The portfolio may go up or down like any other stock portfolio, but you bought it for income, which probably will not change or potentially go up. It is like buying a bond-the interest or coupon from the bond is paid at par ($1,000) regardless what the value of the bond goes to (unless of course the bond defaults), the option income is based on the number of shares you own or individual stocks with call writing options, cash flow is generated from premiums, capital gains, and dividends paid not the portfolio value.

For example, if you had $100,000 in a stock portfolio and $100,000 in an option portfolio (it is still a stock portfolio), they would both go up and down. The regular portfolio would yield around 1.1 percent, which is the average dividend yield, while the option portfolio would yield around 5-6 percent or more, plus capital gains (short-term) any interest accumulated, and you still get the dividend yield. Plus you can offset long-term gains with short-term losses-you can specify to sell at a loss, which gives you more cash that you can reinvest in other options. To illustrate further, the income on the 1.1 percent yield is around $1,100 per year, and the income on the option contract can be $6,000 or more per year. Option funds can generally generate more income because they have more dollars to spend on investments and receive additional in flows of cash. You can purchase equity traded option funds (closed-end) such as FFA, BEP and others.

- *Real estate investment trusts (REITs)* basically fall into two types: equity traded and direct ownership (closed end). All REITs pay out 90 percent of the revenues generated to the investors. Some provide a pass-through for depreciation for tax purposes. Real estate has recently been classified as the fourth asset class and is an asset that's noncorrelated to the stock market. Always check the types of properties inside a REIT. Higher-risk types include shopping malls, strip malls, apartment complexes, etc.; lower-risk types are class A office space with long-term leases and major corporations leasing the properties. Check the lengths and terms of the leases, holding periods for breakeven or redemption; how much leverage they have, meaning how much they borrow to buy the real estate; and whether they are triple-net leases, in which the lessee pays everything. Corporations pay rent from the operating budget, which means that they pay the rent before they pay stockholders or bondholders.

- *Direct-ownership REITs* (closed-end funds) give, in a sense, direct ownership of the real estate purchased inside the fund and pass through a portion of the real estate depreciation to the investor. Most offer a fixed rate of return and potentially increase the yield over time. Average yield is from 6–8 percent annualized and compounded quarterly They are not as liquid, as they generally invest entirely in real estate and offer limited redemption; redemption at death or disability as per social security is usually 100 percent-anything less has a percentage around 10 percent from the NAV.

If the REIT is paying 6 percent, the breakeven point would be around fourteen months. Most REITs have a one-year hold. The NAV[5] is usually fixed unless the funds offer a dividend reinvestment plan, at

---

5   Net asset value

which time you buy more shares for less than the NAV. Closed-end REITs have a life expectancy at which time the investor must vote on what he or she wants to do: keep the income going by extending the fund, liquidate and take cash, or make it a publicly traded equity index fund, all of which is stated in the prospectus. You always need to check on the type of real estate for risk. Shopping malls, hotels, strip malls, and rental properties all generally carry higher risk than class A commercial properties.

TIP: If you want more liquidity and diversification from a closed-end REIT, take the cash dividend and buy an equity traded REIT; you can now have additional growth and or sell off smaller quantities of shares. Understand closed-end REITs before you buy them.

- *Equity-traded REITs* trade like stocks on the open market. They are more volatile and invest in multiple strategies of real estate, hotels, other REITs, and preferred stocks. visit www.nareit.com for more information.

- *1031 real estate transfers* offer tax solutions for real estate investors (if you actually own the real estate) to defer capital gains tax. The IRS code allows a property owner to sell one real estate asset and buy another similar property without incurring (deferring) capital gains tax. Typically individuals with highly appreciated properties where they have a low cost basis and the current value is high from appreciation. An example would be vacant property where you sell non-income-producing land and reinvest into some form of commercial rental income-producing real estate. Always consult a tax adviser, as the rules can get quite complicated.

In simple form, it works like this: You sell your property, and the proceeds go into escrow with a qualified intermediary (most 1031 exchange companies can find you an intermediary). Within forty-five days of the sale of your relinquished property, you must notify the qualified intermediary of the intent to replace your property with the 1031-identified property. The companies will provide lists of properties they have to offer for exchange. If, after forty-five days, you have not identified your replacement property, you pay tax on the sale. Once you identify the replacement property, you sign all the agreements and you start enjoying income from the new property as a landlord, without all the headaches and maintenance. The total process must be completed within a total of 180 days of the final sale of the relinquished property. Always check with your tax adviser and the 1031 exchange company for exit strategies if you wish to sell your share of the newly acquired property. For more information, call 1-800-IRS-1031, search for "1031 exchanges" on the Internet, and for a qualified intermediary.

In addition to the specialty funds just described, there are utility funds, financial services funds, leisure funds, aggressive growth funds, global growth funds, and more than fourteen thousand more mutual funds.

So your job is easy, right? Just pick the right investment options, rebalance all your portfolios, eliminate any overlap from your portfolios, moderate your risk, and maintain good growth potential!

On the next few pages, I'll help you determine the differences, advantages, and disadvantages of various investment products.

10d) Comparing Mutual Funds, Index Funds, ETFs, Money Managers, and Annuities

- *Mutual funds* have been around for over eighty years and allow diversification and ownership of a wide variety of stocks or bonds with small amounts of investment capital. In addition, you get professional money management. The downside is that cost, fees, and commissions can be very high; the higher the turnover (buying and selling), the higher the potential capital gains and commission costs. You need to watch turnover in managers as well. Look at top holdings for any overlap, and watch the cost of fees, commissions, 12b-1 fees, and distribution costs. A good place to start is to check out www.personalfund.com (a paid subscription plan), which offers total cost of ownership and other fund comparisons.

There is also no tax control; you pay capital gains tax every year on the capital gain distribution of the fund, and you receive a step-up in basis because of the tax paid, in nonqualified money. The fund can make money, pass on the capital gains tax to you, and you still could have lost money (not such a good deal). Most individuals repurchase more shares with the gains distributed at the end of the year (both qualified and nonqualified). If the fund's NAV is $10 and it pays a $5 capital gain, your new NAV would be $5; you hope the fund grows in value with the purchase of the additional shares. The fund distributes your tax on a 1099. You can deduct capital losses against capital gains (in nonqualified money) and up to $3,000 to offset ordinary income in any year. Any gain held less than one year is a short-term gain and is taxed at the individual's income tax rate. Any investment sold longer than one year is taxed at the current capital gain rate of 15 percent of your profit.

- *Index funds* follow a particular index like the S&P 500, bond index, Russell 2000, etc. They are passive in nature, meaning that whatever stocks the fund owns, so do you. Index funds are for long-term investors who want to watch their investments grow. Index funds started in 1975, which gives you the opportunity to evaluate their track records. Index fund fees are generally lower than mutual fund fees, because managers only need to track a relatively fixed index of securities. Thus, there is less trading, which gives you a more favorable income tax position, lower realized capital gains tax, lower fees and expenses, and more work by computerization. Over the last twenty years, index funds have outperformed mutual funds by around 2.4 percent.

The average expense ratio for mutual funds was around 1.3 percent, while index funds averaged around 0.2 percent. The differences include the fees that are incurred in mutual funds with sales loads and redemption fees, commissions from turnover of stock, and bond sales.

- *ETFs,* or exchange-traded funds, started on the American Stock Exchange in 1993. They trade like stocks on the open market (every fifteen seconds), generally carry lower commissions, and can be bought on margin or borrowed money, or sold short-a sale of a security not owned by the seller. You can also place limit and stop orders on ETFs. You can write covered options, which could enhance income returns. There are no capital gains, as they are exchanged or transferred, so you control your taxation unlike a mutual fund, which taxes your gains every year. The first ETF (Spiders, with the ticker symbol SPY) is over ten years old and tracks the S&P 500. In addition to Spiders, popular ETF index funds include Diamonds/Dow Jones Industrial Average (symbol DIA) and Qubes (QQQ symbol), which tracks the NASDAQ 100. With ETFs you can diversify into almost ever sector with minimal investment dollars (actually you could buy one share); some energy sectors share funds like the S&P Global Energy (ticker IXC), Dow Jones US Energy IYE, and Gold (GLD). They are traded short and often, so if you're dollar-cost averaging, they may not be right for you; the frequent trading can eat up your investment dollars. You may be better off with a no-load index mutual fund.

The next level for ETFs will be actively managed versus passive baskets of ETFs (like fund of funds). It should be interesting to see how they perform with higher management fees. Go to www.morningstar.com/cover/etf.html or www.sec.gov/answers/indexf.htmfor more information on index and ETF funds.

- *Managed money* includes individual stocks and bonds. In the past, you hired a money manager for around $100,000 investment per manager per asset class or style (large-cap value, mid-cap, and the style might be moderate or aggressive). This was with the idea that he or she would diversify your portfolio and theoretically do a better job than you could because of access to resources. Several problems ensued. First, to diversify into five asset classes, you would need over $500,000 and at least another $500,000+ to invest in hedge funds. Second, each manager didn't know the other existed, so you had potential overlap, and wash sale rules were in effect, which could affect taxation. Third, there was no rebalancing. The money managers kept investing, thinking that this would last forever, which it didn't and that they could beat the benchmarks—meaning that if the S&P 500 was the unmanaged benchmark index and the S&P was down 20 percent and they were down 16 percent, they beat the benchmark. However, you still lost 16 percent while they were slapping hands over their victory and got paid quite nicely. Not so hot for you.

- *New-era managed portfolios* are how I describe a process that, in fairness, some mutual funds also use. Money managers have embraced the concept of combining five to seven asset classes in one account, instead of getting five or more separate and confusing statements for each account, with an overlay manager who makes sure that money managers are talking to each other. This helps eliminate overlap of securities and achieve better diversification. You can now have the benefit of this multiple portfolio management for around $250,000, compared with $500,000-$1 million for the old process of individual managers without the combined asset classes in one account.

Many money managers also do a daily evaluation and rebalancing (see the Thompson report in chapter 10). The accounting world did not embrace this, but the IRS now allows the accountants to attach a broker statement[27] showing all trades and cost basis for profit and loss without the accountants to manually complete this tedious entry work.

Additional advantages of direct money managers include control of the process; the ability to see what the managers are doing on a daily basis with around-the-clock online access, which helps you make decisions for any changes; the ability to make changes immediately to the portfolio; and control of costs meaning you know exactly what you are paying in fees, and the fees are generally tax deductible.

The disadvantage is that you see the fee on a quarterly basis, so you need to get over the impact of this large sum of money being withdrawn from the account. Your mutual funds and other investment vehicles may, and probably do, cost more.

What you *can't* see *can* hurt you. Fees directly affect performance. With the fixed cost, you can quickly determine whether the fee is worth the performance.

- *Annuities* are contracts issued by an insurance company that guarantee the investor will not run out of money through equal payments. Annuities also bypass the probate process, as they are beneficiary-designated products like life insurance, IRAs, etc. Most companies now offer living benefits (a guaranteed percentage, usually around 5% of the transfer value for the rest of your life regardless of the portfolio balance), annual ratchets (or the highest achieved portfolio balance) for death benefits minus any distributions, multiple investment choices, and spousal survivorship rights. This is where on death of the primary annuitant (owner of the contract), the surviving spouse assumes the contract and continues with income payments versus a lump sum distribution. The cost of annuities varies by the goodies you wish to attach to your contract such as estate riders, lifetime income, survivorship, and so on. You need to analyze these costs versus the benefit to you and your family. In essence, an annuity is buying insurance to protect your investment and future income. The annuity can run on an average an additional one percent for the insurance (and can vary by product) above mutual fund expenses—in most cases, it's not a bad deal.

> There is an age-old argument about whether mutual funds should be inside an IRA versus inside an annuity. For example, if you had $1 million in mutual funds in an IRA and $1 million in mutual funds inside an annuity and the day you died, the market crashed and they were both valued at $400,000, the mutual funds would pay $400,000 and the annuity would pay at least $1 million, less any distributions. You make the call.

- By transferring lump-sum distributions from your 401(k), IRA, or pension plans into an annuity, you have now protected your investment with the guaranteed death benefit, which is the dollar amount you transferred into the annuity, offered with annuities, you still have investment choices for future growth, which can give you a raise if your investments go up since the distribution is generally based on a percentage of the total portfolio.

- Pension plans generally give you three choices: 100 percent to you with no survivorship income to your spouse after you die, which is higher income payout; joint, which gives you less money monthly; or lump sum. You work thirty years, and they give you back a fixed amount for as long as you live. Your spouse will receive zero, if the single lifetime income option is chosen, or approximately 40 or 25 percent of that amount on your death if you chose the survivorship option. If you transferred that to an annuity, you would

27   The IRS requires you to record all profit-and-loss transactions on your tax return.

have a guaranteed death benefit, lifetime income stream, and the possibility for a raise because the income is based on a percentage of the total portfolio amount.

- With annuities, unlike life insurance, you do not need to take a physical exam to put money in them and to allow contributions or transfers up to age eighty-five or higher. Most companies require authorization for policies of $1 million or more.

- You have qualified and nonqualified annuities. Most people maximize their 401(k) or IRA, and then add to nonqualified annuities for additional tax-deferred investment growth.

- Current annuity owners with older policies may be better off completing a tax-free 1035 exchange for better products. Be careful that your death benefit is not higher than the portfolio value; once you transfer to a new policy, the dollar amount you transfer is your new dollar amount death benefit. Some companies offer bonus products to offset this. Again, be careful. The CDSC charges can be 8 percent and extend over ten years.[28]

- All annuities (qualified or non-qualified) carry the 10 percent penalty if you take out distribution prior to age 59½. If you are under 59½, you can take distributions under IRS rule 72t. This allows equal periodic payments for a minimum of five years or an attained age of 59½ (without incurring the 10 percent penalty, you pay ordinary income tax)—whichever comes first.

- 403(b) ERISA-approved qualified retirement plans can transfer vested assets to another like annuity product under the IRS 90/24 rule. This may be an advantage, since you pick up the death benefits and better investment options.

- Equity-Index annuities: beware if you are looking for immediate income-it could be ten years or longer before you can actually receive any income. Furthermore, if you take prior distributions, you will probably incur huge penalties. The incentive for agents to sell this type of product is very high commissions. There are much better choices for income: buy bonds (treasury's or other high quality bonds), a variable or fixed annuity, high dividend paying stocks, closed end funds, and/or a combination of investments to help you achieve your income goals.

• Immediate annuities offer immediate payouts of a fixed income amount based on the portfolio size for the rest of your life.

• Variable annuities are generally used when deferred income is needed. The payouts fluctuate by the portfolio size and can offer more income if the underlying funds perform well. Usually variable annuities carry higher costs. You can have split buckets in a variable annuity-part of the money goes to a guaranteed fixed account and part goes to the variable side. What it accomplishes is over a certain period of time the money you put in is the worst you will do.

Annuities require research. Don't be fooled with bells and whistles that have no value to you or your family. Ask what each extra feature costs, what the charges are for early liquidation and how long the charges apply, and what the features do for you. Look at the financial strength of the insurance/annuity company.

Go to www.sec.gov/answers/annuity.htm for more information.

10e) An Example of How I Manage a Client's Money

I start with a minimum of $1 million in investable assets.[29] I utilize a money manager that incorporates all the asset classes into one account such as U.S Large Cap Value, U.S. Small/Mid-Cap Equity, International Equity, REITs, U.S. and International Fixed Income, with added values like market neutral funds and commodity mutual funds. I make sure

28   CDSC charges are back-end sales charges that will be deducted upon termination of the contract prior to its maturity. Class B mutual funds also carry back-end charges.

the money manager incorporates daily evaluations and rebalancing with a conservative-to-moderate investment risk level. This is designed to protect from downsides and give realistic upside potential-around 6–8 percent (or higher) net of all fees. The money manager has nonqualified, tax-efficient portfolios, as well as portfolios designed for qualified plans. We can do a tax-loss selling in non-qualified portfolios to offset any long-term gains. For additional dollars, I diversify with individual money managers (around $100,000 cash per manager) to add more potential growth without adding overlap of investment style or objectives. This allows me to diversify with what I call risk capital (maybe 20–25 percent of the entire portfolio) into hedge funds; managed futures contracts or covered-call writing; REITs, in both equity-traded and closed-end funds; managed bond portfolios; individual bonds, which I like to buy under par at $1,000; short-term adjustable-rate funds; short-term inter-mediate bond funds; closed end income funds; and cash. We also diver-sify their 401K plans with a similar approach by adding a self-directed brokerage account that we can transfer cash or profits from rebalancing the portfolios to purchase additional non-correlated or other invest-ments to help diversify.

Always keep your money earning something. Once a year, and sometimes sooner, I rebalance profit or cash and put it somewhere con-servative. I then take all accounts because they are live feeds from the brokerage, bank, mutual funds, annuities, etc., and consolidate them into one statement reflecting profit/loss, performance, and total net worth at a glance in one combined statement. I help protect my cli-ents' interests with investment policies, risk-tolerance profiles, ongoing due diligence, monitoring of investments and investment returns, and ongoing contact. Open communication ensures long-term relationships and helps build trust.

---

29   This is for educational purposes only and is not intended for a recommen-dation on investments. Consult with your financial adviser or tax adviser, and always read the prospectus before investing.

I like disclosure—no hidden fees or agendas, and no surprises.

If You Don't Have $1 Million

You can accomplish a similar investment strategy with mutual funds. Many funds offer actively managed balanced portfolios similar to the above mentioned money manager, with a blend of all the asset classes, which could be small/mid-cap, value, growth, aggressive growth, income, and bonds, (or you can select criteria that fits your risk level) in one account. Balanced funds are designed to add stability and aid in the selection of the correct asset class and risk profile depending on how aggressive you are. Once you have invested the majority of your money into less risky investments, you can then diversify into alternative non-correlated investments such as fund of funds, equity REITs, closed-end REITs (if you used a closed-end REIT and wanted to add additional diversification and liquidity you could reinvest the dividend into an equity traded or open-end REIT, which trades on an exchange, bond portfolios, ETFs (exchange traded funds) in which you can buy as little as one share, commodity funds, option (covered-call writing) funds, developing markets, closed end income funds, and international funds to spread the risk in your portfolios. You can start out small (approximately $100) with most mutual funds.

You can do small amounts with each of the funds you select and gradually keep adding money to them. The point is that, regardless of how much money you have, you should start something and keep it going!

10f) Arbitration Alert

Important Notice

An important area of concern for the investor is arbitration and mediation. You sign an arbitration clause with a brokerage account, so if you are unhappy with performance, fraud, or improper investments and you sue, you go to arbitration. In rare cases, you can actually sue directly. It costs money out of pocket (sometimes a lot of money), time frames are three years or more to settle, and most companies know the goal of arbitration is to win fifty cents on the dollar-your share, less attorney fees and costs-to get there. Read your arbitration clause, and make sure you have an investment policy in place that spells out your investment objectives and risk-tolerance profiles and guidelines. Also, be sure to monitor your accounts and activity.

Don't be afraid to ask questions on performance, investment selections, and the risk associated with those investments. Always read the prospectus, keep your original trade confirmation tickets, and know what your costs going in and going out are (step 5).

The NASD states that the broker must "know thy client." I say to you: "Know thy broker." Check out your broker at www.finra.com.

10.g) Understanding Mortgages

The first thing you should do is prepare a detailed budget as outlined in Chapter 3, Step 3. Understand what you can afford, then look for a home that matches your finances, and understand the types of mortgages and how they work for the long and short term. Home ownership is one of the largest investments individuals can make, make it good one.

TIP: If you re-finance your home and incur PMI (private mortgage insurance) insurance, after January 1, 2007, it is a taxable deduction.

Let's examine the various types of mortgages: you can go to web site: www.bankrate.com or www.bloomberg.com/market/rates[30] to see various types of mortgages, indexes, current rates, and a calculators to play with.

Types of Indexes

Lenders base the interest rates they charge using the following most common indexes which are the 1-year constant maturity Treasury securities (CMT), the Cost of Funds Index (COFI), and the London Interbank offered rate (LIBOR). Some lenders use their own cost of funds as an index. The lender then adds a margin to the index which equals your loan interest rate. *An example*: Index is 4% + margin of 3% = Fully indexed rate of 7%. Your FICA score will influence your margin rate. Your payments would generally change with the interest rate up or down, your margin would remain the same. You should always ask (show me) how each of these indexes have fluctuated in the past, and where it is published for you to see. You can find a lot of information in the newspapers or on the Internet.

Reverse mortgages allow homeowners aged sixty-two and older to take the equity from their homes. No loan payments are due until the home is sold or the homeowner dies (the beneficiaries receive the additional appreciation above the purchase contract-if any). There is no taxation on the money you receive, and you can take a lump-sum payment, installments, or a combination. Reverse mortgages can be very expensive and require a lot of research. Fannie Mae (HECM) offers reverse mortgages that the government insures. Consult your tax adviser to see whether reverse mortgages can help you obtain additional money for retirement. These are usually for individuals who are real-estate rich and cash poor. Visit http://www.hud.gov/offices/hsg/sfh/hecm/rmtopten.cfm for more information.

Fixed rate mortgages are exactly that, fixed for the life of the loan, 10, 15, 20, and 30-year terms are the most common. The rate follows the 10-year Treasury bond. The least risky.

Interest only ARM mortgages, you pay interest only on your balance. Your payment is much lower than a fixed rate or traditional ARM, as an example-$100,000 mortgage balance at 6% interest only would be 100,000 x 6% = $6000 year divided by 12 = $500 per month approximate payment plus taxes, insurance, etc. However, if you put down each month a principal reduction, it reduces your interest and mortgage by that amount each month. It allows you to control your payment amount and how fast you want to pay off your loan. They generally offer 1, 3, 5, 7, and 10-year fixed interest only lock in periods with a 30-year amortization of the loan. After that the loan adjusts generally every 6 months to the current market rates following prime rate (the rate banks lend their best customers) or Libor (London Interbank Offered Rate-which is a daily rate that banks offer to lend unsecured loans to other banks in the London wholesale money market) and usually have a cap on how high they can go-and how fast. Keep in mind that your payment will start to increase when the loan resets, that is because you must start paying back principal as well.

Tip:

go to: http://www.federalreserve.gov/pubs/arms/arms_english.htm or www.federalreserve.gov click on financial education/home ownership/mortgages for consumer handbook on ARM's

ARM's are probably one of the most confusing and mis-understood mortgages (also the most abuse to the consumer).

Adjustable rate mortgages the interest rate changes periodically, usually in relation to one of the indexes mentioned above. and your payments can go up or down according to that specific index. The terms

---

30   Permission granted from Bloomberg to offer link to Bloomberg web page as noted above

are usually limited period of time (adjustment period) ranging from 1 month to 5 years or more. When looking at ARM's the interest may be lower than a fixed rate initially, so you need to ask yourself several questions:

• How long am I going to be in this house? Can I afford the payments if the interest rate goes to 8% or higher?
• What is the lifetime cap on this loan?
• What is the rate cap and or payment when my loan resets at the end of the initial term?
• What is the maximum your rate can adjust up or down from one adjustment period to the next?
• What is the lifetime cap on the interest for the loan? By law all ARM's must have a lifetime cap.
• Is this a carryover loan for rates? Which means it is not fully indexed and your payment may actually go up even though rates have declined or stayed the same.
• Is this a balloon ARM?
• Is this a limited payment option mortgage? You choose the payment or interest; any amount you do not pay gets added to the loan amount for future payments. They recalculate generally every 5 years. You could end up owing more than you started with. And a lot higher payment.
• Does this loan have a prepayment penalty?
• Are there points in this loan?
• Is the risk worth the initial lower rate and payment? Risk can be deceiving as evidenced by the major downturn in the housing market, some housing prices are significantly lower than a year ago, so if you were planning on a short term and sell the house, you may not be able to because you paid more for the house than what is currently worth-if you bought a house now because of low rates and pricing, think about where interest rates are going in the future.

Always look at your APR vs. your interest rate-the APR is your actual cost of money for the loan. If it is higher by a lot, then so probably is your monthly payment when it resets. Most lenders want 20% down payment or they charge you PMI insurance[31] (it is tax deductible after January 1st, 2007). You need to do your homework, buying a home is a major decision; make sure it is a good one for a long time. Get information in writing before you pay any fees. Nothing happens until you fill out an application, they review your credit history (FICA), and an appraisal is complete. They can promise you anything-until these items are complete-nothing happens!

For more information you can call the U.S Department of Housing and Urban Development toll-free at 1 800-569-4287 or go to www. hud.gov to speak with financial advisors, housing councilors, and more information.

Each year you can receive a free credit report form any of the following agencies: www.equifax.com www.expierian.com www.transunion. com

Call for identity theft and register for FREE fraud alert, fraud alerts are good for 90 days, and then you must renew your alert. If you had identity theft YOU MUST fill out a police report, then register your fraud alert, which will stay on the reporting agencies for 7 years.

To report fraud toll free numbers: (FREE)
Equifax: 1-800-525-6285
Expierian: 1-888-397-3742
TransUnion: 1-800-680-7289

Tip: Most individuals do not realize the new law (HPA-homeowners protection act of 1998) gives you the right to cancel PMI insurance when your mortgage meets the required 80% of value. The lender must discloseatcloing.http://www.frbsf.org/publications/consumer/pmi.html for more information

10g) Mortgage Shopping Worksheet[32]

Ask your lender or broker to help you fill out worksheet

	FIXED RATE	ARM 1	ARM 2	ARM 3
Name of lender/contact information				
Mortgage amount				
Loan term (e.g., 15,30 year				
Loan description				
(fixed rate, 3/1 ARM, interest only ARM				

graduated payment or stepped-rate mortgages use ARM columns)

Basic Features for Comparison

Fixed rate interest rate/APR
(use ARM columns for graduated payments)

ARM initial interest rate and APR

How long does the initial rate apply?
What is the interest rate after the initial period?

ARM features

How often can the rate adjust?
What is the index and what is the current rate?

Interest Rate Caps

What is the periodic interest rate cap?
What is the lifetime interest rate cap?
How high can the rate go?
How low can the rate go?
What is the payment cap?
Can this loan have a negative amortization?
What is the limit to how much the balance
  can grow ?
Before the loan will be recalculated?
Is there a prepayment penalty if I pay off
the mortgage early?
How long is the prepayment penalty?
How much is it?
Is there a balloon payment on this mortgage?
If so, what is the estimated amount and when
Would it be due?

31   PMI insurance-Private Mortgage Insurance, it is a fee charged to homeowners that do not have the required 20% down payment for a mortgage.

What are the estimated origination fees
and charges for this loan?   _____ _____ _____ _____
Are there any points on this loan?   _____ _____ _____ _____

Monthly Payment Amounts

What will the monthly payments be for
the first year of the loan?   _____ _____ _____ _____
Does this include taxes and insurance?   _____ _____ _____ _____
Condo or homeowner's association fees?   _____ _____ _____ _____
If not, what are the estimates for these amounts? _____ _____ _____ _____
What will my monthly be after 12 months
if the index rate Stays the same?   _____ _____ _____ _____
Goes up 2%   _____ _____ _____ _____
Goes down 2%?   _____ _____ _____ _____
What is the most my minimum monthly
payment could be: _____ _____ _____ _____
What is the least my payment could be?   _____ _____ _____ _____
After 1 year?   _____ _____ _____ _____
After 3 years?   _____ _____ _____ _____
After 5 years?   _____ _____ _____ _____

---

32   From the consumer Handbook on Adjustable rate Mortgages by the Federal
Reserve Board and the Office of Thrift Supervision.

Chapter XI

All About Bonds

People don't buy bonds to get rich; they buy bonds to stay rich[33].

In my opinion, you should buy bonds when they are below par ($1,000). If you buy at $900 and if the government agency, municipality, or company calls the bond, it is generally called "at par." This means you get the income from the coupon plus the capital gain from the cost less the sale price of $1,000 minus $900 cost = $100 gain, which also increases your yield. The lower the price of the bond, the higher the yield. Always check the yield to maturity and the yield to call on a bond. The coupon is your interest you collect from the par value (1,000 x 6 percent coupon is 60 per bond). The yield is what you make at maturity or early redemption that is your real return.

TIP: The next item for attention is doing a bid/ask into the secondary market before you buy. This does 2 things: one, it lets you know if there is a secondary resale market, and two, it tells what your bond is generally worth if you sell before maturity.

All bonds have similar characteristics. They represent the indebtedness, or liability, of their issuers in return for a specified sum, or principal. All debt has a maturity date, which is from one day to thirty years. Short-term debt is generally under one year to maturity, intermediate debt is one to ten years, and long-term debt is generally ten years or more. The bondholders receive a fixed interest rate usually for the lifetime of the bond duration. This is called the coupon rate. The rate of return for the interest is calculated two ways: current yield, which is the annual flow of interest or income, or yield to maturity, if the bond is held to maturity and redeemed at par value. Each debt agreement has obligations that must be met (stated in the legal documents), including the date of maturity, coupon rate, pledges of collateral, and any other conditions that must be met.

There are two types of bonds. *Bearer bonds* are coupon bonds that anybody can cash, since there are no names on the bonds to identify ownership. *Registered bonds* are issued in certificate form in the owner's name and are held in street name if in a brokerage account. All bonds carry ratings established by Moody's and Standard & Poor's. The ratings reflect the risk of owning the bonds: Moody's ratings are Aa3. A1, A2, Ba2; Standard & Poor's ratings are AA+, A, BBB+. Non-rated bonds are typically small municipalities or projects that cannot afford the cost of obtaining a rating from one of the rating agencies.

Bonds carry risk of default, price fluctuations (if interest rates rise, bond prices fall; if interest rates fall, bond prices rise), and risk of inflation (not keeping up with inflation versus interest received). Most bonds have a *call* feature that allows their redemption prior to maturity. When you buy bonds, buy for yield, which is your true return. You need to look at yield to maturity and yield to call. The coupon or interest rate is based on par or $1,000, so if your coupon is 6 percent, your interest received would be $60 per bond, generally paid every six months.

Bonds trade with interest to the settlement date unless otherwise stated. Corporate, municipal, and agency bond interest is based on a 30-day month and a 360-day calendar year.

33   As far as I know this is my original quote

Calculating bond yields:
Annual interest $70

$$\frac{\text{Annual interest } \$70}{\text{Current market price } \$1,000} = \text{Current yield } 7\%$$

Calculating taxable yields:
Taxable equivalent = Tax-exempt yield

$$\frac{\text{Tax-exempt yield}}{\text{Yield}} \quad 100\% \text{ tax bracket}$$

In other words, if your tax-exempt yield is 4 percent and your tax bracket is 31 percent

$$\frac{4\% \text{ Tax-exempt Yield}}{100\%-31\%} = \frac{4}{69\%} = .0579 (5.58)$$

Calculating Bond Quote Pricing

Quotes are expressed as a percentage of face value or par amounts of $1,000. They are quoted in increments of eighths of $10: 1/8 of $10 = 1.25 or $1.25. So a quote of 90-1/8 of par would be $901.25. As mentioned previously, when buying bonds, you should look at the resale market, or secondary market, before you buy. You can have your financial adviser put in a bid-ask on the bond, which will provide you with the cost basis and whether there is a secondary market for resale.

To find your tax equivalent the easy way, use the following tables:

Tax-free Yield

3.50%	4.00%	4.50%	5.00%	5.50%	6.00%	6.50%	7.00%

Federal
Income Tax
Bracket[34] **Taxable Equivalent**

15%	4.12%	4.71%	5.29%	5.88%	6.47%	7.06%	7.64%	8.24%
25%	4.66%	5.33%	6.00%	6.67%	7.33%	8.00%	8.67%	9.00%
28%	4.86%	5.56%	6.25%	6.94%	7.64%	8.33%	9.03%	9.72%
33%	5.22%	5.97%	6.71%	7.46%	8.20%	8.95%	9.70%	10.40%
35%	5.34%	6.15%	6.92%	7.69%	8.46%	9.23%	10.00%	10.76%

Tax-loss Worksheet

Par value	Description	Coupon	Maturity	CUSIP#	Cost basis
————	————	————	————	————	————
————	————	————	————	————	————

Settlement date (when the bond settles for payment of sale or purchase)

————————   ————————

Swap summary:	Sale side	Buy side	Net change
Par value	————	————	————
Annual income	————	————	————
Average coupon	————	————	————
Average maturity	————	————	————
Average price	————	————	————
Average yield	————	————	————
Principal proceeds	————	————	————
Tax loss or gain	————		

Bond swaps are when a bond is sold and the proceeds are used to buy another bond. Investors can sell a lower-coupon bond at a loss for tax purposes and buy a similar discounted bond with the proceeds. You are allowed up to $3,000 per year of losses to offset gains against ordinary income, carried forward each year until depleted. This allows the investor to remain in the same investment and tax-free income position, and it allows a loss to offset the gains in other securities. Bond swaps help improve the portfolio and increase quality or income.

A wash sale occurs when you sell a bond and buy another bond that is substantially similar within sixty-one days of the sale (thirty days prior and thirty days after the sale). A wash applies to losses. Check with your tax adviser, because you could lose the tax loss and have a reportable gain.

For bond research tools, visit the following Web sites: www.investinginbonds.com, www.treasurydirect.gov, and www.bondschool.com. www.bloomberg.com

Municipal bonds, known as muni bonds, are the debt obligation of a state or local government. The funds raised support governmental needs or special projects. They can be insured against default or not. Some of the insurers are MBIA, AMBAC, and FGIC.

Always ask if the municipal bond has an AMT in it. Even tax-free money markets are not always tax free; some of the interest may be subject to the AMT.

Types of Municipal Bonds

- *Public purpose municipal bonds* are issued for government needs such as roads, schools, and municipal buildings. The interest income is tax free.

- *Nonpurpose municipal bonds* are issued for nongovernment purposes, such as student loans and low-income housing.

---

34   The amount is 10 percent for the first $6,000 of taxable income for singles, then $7,000 after 2007, $12,000 for married couples filing jointly, then $14,000 after 2007. The remainder of income goes to 15 percent, 25 percent, 28 percent, 33 percent, and 35 percent maximum.

The interest is free from regular income tax but is subject to the AMT.

- *Taxable municipal bonds*, commonly referred to as industrial revenue bonds, are issued for nongovernmental purposes, such as loans to farmers and recreational facilities. They are taxable as regular income.

- *Muni bonds* are sold at a capital gain or capital loss just like a stock or mutual fund; secondary market resale determines the cost basis. A bond held to maturity results in a capital gain.

- *General obligation muni bonds* are bonds for which the principal and interest payments are secured by the full faith, credit, and taxing power of the issuing state or local government.

- *Revenue bonds* are backed directly by the revenues of a particular project, such as bridges and roads.

Insured muni bonds offer a high degree of credit safety. If the issuer of the insured bonds defaults, the insurance company agrees to pay both the principal and interest when due.

- *Bond funds* are typically managed for total return; managing for yield is more directly related to income.

- *Prerefunded muni bonds* are good for security; the U.S. government secures most of them.

- *Zero-coupon muni bonds* do not pay interest. They are sold at a deep discount to face value, and you collect interest and principal at maturity.

- *Taxable Zero* coupon bonds are sold at a deep discount and do not pay interest, they accrue until maturity and pay par value upon redemption. IRS taxes the interest every year as though you received it.

- *Original issue discount (OID) bonds* purchased at original issue discount give the original purchaser a tax-free capital gain if held to maturity. Selling the bond before maturity gives the owner a tax-free capital gain for the period held. You must accrete the amount using the following formula:

Consider a ten-year original issue discount bond at $900 (par is $1,000). You hold the bond for five years and sell the bond at $960 for a profit of $60.

$100 discount divided by 10 years = $10 accreted interest
Profit $60
$10 per year × 5 years held   -$50
Capital gain on sale $10

If the bond were sold below $950 ($900 plus accreted interest), it would be a deductible loss.

OID bonds require the owner to include a prorated portion of the discount earned (accreted) for the period held as ordinary income each year. You must file IRS form 1099-OID, which indicates the amount to include in income. This adjusts the cost basis each year so that you are not taxed twice.

The first rule of thumb when buying municipal bonds is to look at the state in which you live. If you buy within your state, the interest is generally tax free at all levels; otherwise, you may be subject to state taxation.

The second rule is: before you buy a bond, put in a bid-ask. This gives you two things—a secondary market for resale and the market price, or cost basis.

- *Municipal bond funds* invest in tax-exempt bonds issued by states, cites, and local governments. Look for an AMT, as the interest may be taxable under the AMT rule.

AMT, as mentioned earlier, is the alternative minimum tax. Interest is subject to the AMT. You should always ask whether the bonds contain AMT, including muni bond funds and tax-free money market funds. They may have as much as 25 percent or more reportable AMT income.

You can search for AMT on the Internet to learn more about the importance of understanding how the tax works (for income tax).

Other Types of Bonds, Including Government and Corporate Bonds

U.S. treasury bonds offer the highest degree of creditworthiness. Timely payments of interest and principal are guaranteed by the full faith of the federal government. Treasury bonds have locked-in interest rates, and the interest is exempt from state and local taxes. Most treasury bonds cannot be called prior to maturity and have an attractive secondary market resale mostly because of the no-call feature and high liquidity.

Types of Treasury Bonds

- *Treasury notes* are intermediate-term bonds that are issued in one-to ten-year maturity, and denominations (face values) are $1,000-$100,000.

- *Treasury bonds* are long-term bonds that mature in ten years or longer. They are issued in denominations of $1,000-$1 million.

- *Treasury bills* are sold at a discount through treasury auctions. The bonds go to the highest bidder and mature in three to twelve months. They are issued in denominations of $1,000-$1 million.

- *Treasury inflation indexed securities (TIPS)* are indexed to the consumer price index (CPI). The interest stays the same from original purchase; however, the bond value increases to the inflation rate of the CPI. You can receive higher value, but you cannot receive less than par of $1,000.

- *Collateralized mortgage obligations (CMOs)* are backed by the broad diversification of several mortgage pools, which helps reduce the risk of prepayment by homeowners. Maturity and yield are hard to calculate, as they are ever-moving targets. The underlying pools are backed by a government agency and guarantee timeliness of payments and principal only. They receive the same ratings as other bonds or Government National Mortgage Association (GNMA) and come in denominations of $1,000.

- *Series EE bonds* are appreciation bonds sold at a discount basis (50 percent of face value). They pay no interest but increase in value until maturity. You can redeem them prior to maturity. You can declare an annual increase in the value of the bond as ordinary income each year, or you can defer taxes until redemption.

- *Series H bonds* are ten-year bonds issued in exchange for Series E or EE bonds in denominations of $500, $1,000, $5,000, or $10,000. They are issued and redeemed at par and pay semiannual interest over the ten-year period. They are subject to federal income tax but do not require state or local taxes.

- *Series I bonds* pay two rates of interest: one rate that changes with the rate of inflation and one rate that is fixed. They are sold at face value, which means a $100 face-value bond will cost you $100, and earn interest throughout the thirty-year maturity. You pay federal income tax but no state or local taxes.

Corporate Bonds

Companies issue debt (bonds) to raise capital versus issuing additional stock. Bonds do not dilute ownership like the sale of stock. Secured bondholders of the debentures are banks and other institutions that hold collateral, or hard assets, in case of default. You need to look at the underlying strength of the company before you buy stock or bonds. Follow the order of claims priority for payment from companies that default:

- Secured bondholder

- Debenture holders and general creditors
- Subordinated debenture holders
- Preferred stockholders
- Common stockholders

Below are types of corporate bonds:

- *Serial bonds* are issued by corporations to finance a specific use. Company equipment is pledged as collateral.
- *Convertible bonds* offer a conversion to common stock. They have longer maturity dates and are generally callable. If the bond is called, the owner must convert the bond to stock. For example, a $1,000 bond with a conversion of $20 per share would give you 50 shares of common stock (1,000 divided by 20 per share = 50 shares).
- *Convertible preferred stock* is used primarily in takeovers of corporations. The IRS has determined that since this is an exchange in securities rather than a sale, there is no capital gains tax due. The winning company generally issues or tenders convertible preferred stock with attractive yields to entice stockholders to exchange their shares.
- *Corporate bonds* are callable bonds issued by corporations, generally with longer-term maturity dates. If the corporation issues more stock, it could dilute the ownership of existing shareholders. Instead of borrowing from the bank, the company borrows from the public by issuing bonds with attractive yields. The bonds are senior to common stock for security of ownership.
- *Corts (trust preferred securities)* are a hybrid of preferred stock. Companies issue subordinated debt to a trust and deduct the interest payments (versus no deduction for stock dividends). This improves their balance sheets without

diluting stock value or adding debt because they are issuing shares to the trust. They usually have a face value of $25 per share and trade on the open market. For more information go to: http://www.secinfo.com/d1zj61.382.htm.

Look at bonds as part of an overall strategy. Since the early 1900s, a pure bond portfolio has never outperformed a pure equity portfolio. You need a mix of quality equities and quality bonds, and a mix of alternative investments.

Chapter XII

How to Choose an Adviser

The first thing you need to do before selecting an adviser is to determine your goals. Using your budget/retirement, budget/estate worksheets in this book will help you interview potential brokers/bankers who wish to vie for your money. Have them explain how they get paid—by commission, fee only, advisory fees, or a combination. You want no surprises. Ask if they have an investment policy, what their education is, what licenses they hold, what designations they have, what their specialty is, and what their arbitration requirements are (if they have standard or triple arbitration, and so on). After you are comfortable with the answers, ask for a full proposal in writing for an estate plan, retirement plan, investment strategy, insurance quotes, and tax planning. Ask about any Web pages that have financial calculators for you to use. Here are some Web pages you can use to check out the adviser:

www.finra.com	National Association of Securities Dealers
www.cfp.net	Certified Financial Planner Board of Standards
www.naic.org	National Association of Insurance Commissioners
www.sec.gov	Securities and Exchange Commission
www.adviser.sec.gov	SEC investment adviser public disclosure
www.nicep.org	National Institute of Certified Estate Planners
www.iarfc.org	International Association of Registered Financial

Consultants

- *Certified financial planners (CFPs)* are individuals who have passed various tests and have conformed to the CFP board's code of ethics.

- *Certified estate planners (CEPs)* are individuals who have passed various tests and have complied with a code of ethics. They are required to maintain additional and ongoing certified estate courses.

- *Registered investment advisers (RIAs)* must complete ADV forms and register with the SEC for full disclosure and history of the company and the individual. RIA is not a designation and must be spelled out on any form of communication.

- *Chartered life underwriters (CLUs)* are insurance salespersons.

- *Chartered financial consultants (CHFCs)* are insurance agents entering into the financial marketplace.

- *Charted financial analysts (CFAs)* are generally securities analysts who work for larger institutions.

- *Certified public accountants (CPAs)* are tax specialists who are required to have a formal education and maintain ongoing certified estate education.

- *Registered financial consultants (RFCs)* require ongoing certified estate testing.

Do your homework, follow through, and check out your advisers to make sure they are legitimate and what they say they are.

Chapter XIII

Did You Know?
A Little Trivia

- Using margins on broker accounts is just borrowing against your securities held in the account. Generally you can borrow up to 50 percent of your portfolio with specified break points on interest rates.

- Selling short is a sale of a security not owned by the seller (you). You borrow the security (stocks) from your broker, and you repay with shares, not cash. The stock must be in a margin account. For example, if you are betting the stock will go down, you would sell short (borrow) at $60 per share. If the market declines, you buy at $40 per share on the open market and repay the stock to the broker, profiting $20 per share.

- "Short against the box" was originally called so because investors used to keep their investments in a box at home.

- Rule 72 is a rule of thumb to calculate how long it will take to double your money. If your money is earning 6 percent, divide 6 into 72 = 12 years. Substitute any percentage into the 72 to see how long it will take for the return.

- Fixed mortgage rates are generally tied to the ten-year Treasury bond.

- Adjustable rate mortgages, home equity lines, and credit lines follow the prime rate.

- The prime rate is the rate that banks charge their best customers; it usually follows the federal fund discount rate and affects auto loans, home equity loans, and corporate credit lines. The rate is controlled by the banks and reflects the federal discount rate (what banks charge each other for overnight loans).

- The Federal Open Market Committee (FOMC) is the Federal Reserve policy-making division. It is the fluctuating rate that banks charge each other for overnight loans. The banks adjust the prime rate along with the federal discount rate, controlling the rate for slowing the economy and fighting inflation. The primary long-term inflation tracker for the Fed is the CPI. You can track the CPI on the Bureau of Labor Statistics Web site at www.bls.gov/cpi/home.htm.

- Certificates of deposit, or CDs, follow the federal fund discount rate. For more information, visit www.bankrate.com.

- Bond rates are affected by inflation, interest rates, federal fund rates, and consumer and investor confidence.

- Credit card interest rates follow the prime rate.

- 100 basis points equal 1 percentage point.

Chapter XIV

Quick Reference List of Web Pages

www.lifehappens.org	Life insurance calculator
www.irs.gov	Internal Revenue Service
www.irs.gov/govts	Federal/state/local Web pages
www.bankrate.com	Compare all types of interest, mortgages, CDs, calculators, credit lines, and more
www.ssa.gov	Social security
www.medicare.gov	Medicare
www.adviserinfo.sec.gov	Investment adviser public disclosure
www.irahelp.com	Investments
www.morningstar.com	Mutual fund rating
www.personalfund.com	Mutual fund rating
www.investinginbonds.com	All about bonds
www.bondschool.com	Education on bonds
www.finra.com	National Association of Securities Dealers
www.andrewtobias.com	Mutual fund ratings
www.findlaw.com	National legal Web site
www.giftlaw.com	Gifting
www.treasurydirect.gov	Buying U.S. treasury bonds direct
www.publicdebt.treas.org	A Web page for debt, legal, and other services

www.bls.gov/cpi/home.htm	Bureau of Labor Statistics (tracking the CPI)
www.savingforcollege.com	A college 529 Web page
www.cnnmoney.com	A financial Web page
www.sec.gov/cgi-bin/srch-edgar	Securities and Exchange Commission (SEC); unaudited mutual fund, annuity, and company information Web page
www.lightstonereit.com	REIT Web page
www.ipx1031.com	1031 exchange intermediary
www.amex.com	American Stock Exchange (for options and other investment information)
www.nyse.com	New York Stock Exchange
www.sec.org	Securities and Exchange Commission
www.nfa.futures.org	National Futures Association
www.cftc.gov	Commodities Futures Trading Commission
www.sec.gov/answers/annuity.htm	SEC Web page for annuities
www.horizoninvestments.com	Dynamic asset allocation money manager
www.ira.com	IRA Web page information
www.bigcharts.com	A stock tracking site
www.nicep.org	National Institute of Certified Estate Planners
www.iarfc.org	International Association of Registered Financial Consultants
www.iuniverse.com	My book publisher
www.nareit.com	National Association of REITs
http://www.hud.gov/offices/hsg/sfh/hecm/rmtopten.cfm	Reverse mortgage Web page

www.ici.org	Investment Company Institute (investor mutual fund)
www.acli.org	American Council of Life Insurance
www.nlm.nih.gov/medlineplus/ nursing homes.html	National Library of Medicine
www.medicare.gov/nhcompare /home.asp	U.S. Department of Health and Human Resources
www.bookworm.tv	My web page
www.bloomberg.com	Investment web site

Chapter XV

Summary

Trust is a word used quite often in financial conversations. At some point you do need to trust someone, so how about trusting yourself?

Understanding your investments, good research, and diversification of products as well as diversification of strategies will give you the confidence to help insure your success! Take the emotion out of investing-as in "I love this stock and I don't want to sell it"-and make it a profit decision. Continually monitor your investments. And always have an exit strategy.

The bottom line is this: regardless of whether you invest in money managers, mutual funds, bonds, WRAP, commission programs, options, commodities, or annuities, know what your costs are, know your investment style and risk category, and make sure you have an investment policy in place. Let's keep the interests of all parties where they should be: on you and better performance.

The more you learn, the more you earn, and the more you keep what you've earned.

"Life is more enjoyable when you can afford it"

Glossary

Estate and Financial Definitions

Estate Definitions

A/B trust: Also called a marital trust or bypass trust. A trust to place your unified credit exemption. The A trust is for a living spouse; the B trust is for a deceased spouse.

administrator: Person the court names to administer the estate.

adjusted gross income (AGI): Income less adjustments.

alternate beneficiary: Person who receives assets if the primary beneficiary dies.

alternate valuation date: Date that is not to exceed six months after the date of death. The value of the assets must be lower than, and result in, a reduction of the gross estate to qualify.

alternative minimum tax (AMT): A tax calculation to ensure that individuals and trusts do not escape federal tax liabilities. You or your tax adviser needs to calculate regular income tax and AMT and pay the highest tax.

ancillary administration: Probate of property or assets in another state (unless in trust).

annual exclusion: The annual amount in each taxable year that you may gift to an individual. As of December 31, 2001, this was $11,000 per individual, $22,000 per married couple filing jointly.

asset allocation: The proper investment mix for an investor, based on time frames, goals, needs, objectives, and risk tolerances.

assignment: Transferring your interest in any asset to another party. Used commonly in trusts.

basis: What you paid for an asset. Determines taxes for gains and losses.

beneficiaries: The individuals or corporations that receive assets from the estate after probate or from trust.

bequest: A specific gift by will of a designated class or kind of property.

certificate of trust: Verification of the trust. It explains the powers of the trustee and identifies any successor trustees.

charitable gift: Gifts of cash or property to a qualified charity in which the donor receives tax deductions, income, and estate and capital gains benefits.

Class A beneficiary: Examples are mother, husband, wife, father, son, daughter.

Class B beneficiary: Examples are cousin, aunt, uncle, nephew.

codicil: An amendment to a will.

conservator: An individual (guardian) legally responsible for the care of another individual.

contest: To dispute the terms of a will.

corporate trustee: An institution that manages assets for a trust.

corpus: The principal property of a trust.

creditor: The individual or corporation that is owed money.

Crummey power: The power held by the beneficiary to withdraw a certain amount of money annually from the trust.

custodian: The individual who manages assets for minors under the Uniform Gift to Minors Act (UGMA).

defined benefit plan: A corporate-sponsored retirement plan.

defined contribution plan: An employee-funded retirement plan, sometimes matched by the employer-e.g, 401(k), 403(b).

disclaimer provision: The allowance of the beneficiary (generally the surviving spouse) to refuse acceptance of certain assets for federal tax purposes.

durable power of attorney (financial): Allows full or partial authority of an individual to make decisions and transact business on your behalf in the case of incapacitation. The appointment can be by will provisions, trust instruments, or court appointment.

durable power of attorney (health care): Allows full or partial authority of an individual to make decisions for health care in the event that you are unable to do so (you are incapacitated). The appointment can be by will provisions, trust instruments, or court appointment.

dynasty trust: An irrevocable life insurance trust (ILIT) used by wealthy individuals to create a nontaxable generation, skipping transfers for several generations.

equity: The current net value of an asset.

employer stock option plan (ESOP): A defined contribution plan investing in the employer's stock.

estate: The total value of all assets of an individual or individuals. Used to determine estate taxes and state death taxes as determined by an independent appraiser for IRS purposes.

estate taxes: Federal taxation on the assets in an estate less the unified credits and debts. Federal estate taxes are net; state death taxes are from the gross estate.

executor: The person or institution named to carry out the instruction set forth in the will or trust instrument.

fiduciary: The person or institution that has the legal right to act for another person, generally in financial matters.

funding: The process of transferring assets into your trust.

gain: The difference between what you paid for an asset and what you sold it for (capital gain).

generation-skipping transfer (GST): An exemption that allows you to transfer property or cash for two or more generations for inheritance purposes. This is currently at $1.1 million each (indexed for inflation).

generation-skipping transfer tax: A transfer tax assessed on gifts in excess of $1.1 million to grandchildren and great-grandchildren. The tax is at 55 percent.

gift exclusion: The annual amount allowed per individual to gift to another individual in each calendar year (currently $12,000 for individuals, $24,000 for married couples filing jointly). Commonly used to fund GST, legacy trusts, and life insurance trusts or Crummey trusts.

gift tax: A 55 percent tax (gradually lowering to 35 percent by 2009) that the IRS imposes on any gift exceeding the annual gift exclusion (currently $12,000 per year per person to anybody). Penalties can range from 200–400 percent, plus the current percent gift tax.

grantor: The person who establishes the trust. Also called the donor.

heir: An individual entitled by law to receive part or all of an estate.

incapacity: The state of an individual who is no longer capable of handling his or her own affairs for medical or financial reasons. This can be permanent or temporary. It generally requires court intervention and supervision to protect the individual from wrongdoing.

inheritance: The assets received from the net proceeds from an estate.

inter vivos: A trust established while you are alive.

irrevocable life insurance trust (ILIT): A trust established to own life insurance policies and remove them from your taxable estate. It provides tax-free and estate tax-free dollars to your beneficiaries.

irrevocable trust: A trust that cannot be revoked or cancelled.

intestate: Without a will.

joint tenants with rights of survivorship (JTWROS): Property that transfers automatically to the surviving spouse. The assets are now taxable in the surviving spouse's estate.

living will: A will that states whether or not you wish to be kept alive by artificial means if permanently injured or ill.

Medicaid: A federal program in which you trade assets for nursing home care.

Medicare: A federal health care program for individuals over sixty-five who are covered by social security.

pour-over will: A will stating that any assets left outside your living trust will become part of your living trust.

power of attorney: A legal document giving an individual or corporation power to transact business on your behalf.

probate: The court process of validating your will, paying debts, and distributing assets according to the wishes of your will.

qualified terminal interest property trust (QTIP): Assets transfer into the QTIP trust on the death of the donor and provide income for the surviving spouse. It assures that the remaining assets will transfer to the rightful heirs.

qualified personal residence trust (QPRT): The QPRT trust holds the title to the donor's primary residence (or vacation home), and the donor retains the right to live there for a specified period of time. It removes the property from the estate.

revocable trust: A trust that allows the donor to change, revoke, or cancel the trust any time.

special needs trust: A trust established to take care of an individual who is not capable of doing so for himself or herself.

spendthrift trust: A trust that protects assets from creditors and restricts or limits spending by the beneficiary.

state death tax: A death tax imposed on estates in addition to federal estate taxes.

step-up in basis: An asset that has passed through probate or from a trust. The new value is considered the new "basis" moving forward for tax purposes for the heirs. Generally, it avoids capital gains and gift taxation after passing through probate or from a trust.

successor trustee: The individual or institution that takes over as trustee should the first trustee die, resign, or become incapacitated.

testamentary trust: An unfunded trust inside a will. It does not avoid probate and could trigger gift and capital gains taxes.

testate: Having died with a will.

testator: An individual who leaves a will in force at death.

trustee: An individual or institution that manages and distributes assets for another, or for oneself as in the case of a revocable living trust.

unified credit: The exclusion from federal estate taxes ($675,000 in 2001, $1 million in 2002, increasing to $3.5 million by 2009, back to $1 million in 2011).

will: A written legal document administered and distributed through the probate process, according to your instructions.

Financial Definitions

AON: All-or-none orders are limit orders in which you want to fill the entire order or none of it.

annual report: A document that summarizes the operations and performance of a company for its fiscal year. By law, the report must contain the company's business and disclose its income, profits, losses, and net worth.

annuity: A contract sold by an insurance company that guarantees the annuitant (owner), or his or her beneficiaries, a series of fixed or variable payments.

arbitrage: Profiting from buying a security that costs less than normal and immediately selling it for profit.

asset allocation: Placing several asset classes of investments to offset volatility.

basis point: 100 basis points are equal to 1 percentage point.

bear market: A period of declining stock values.

benchmark: A standard, such as the S&P 500, for money managers or mutual funds to measure their success.

bonds: Fixed income securities that are loans by the investors to companies and governments in return for a fixed amount of payments and agreed interest (coupon rate). The yield is the actual amount you get when held to maturity; if a bond is called early, the yield to call price is your real return.

book value: The difference between what a company owns and what it owes.

bull market: A period of rising stock market values.

capital gain: Money earned on the sale of an asset (selling price minus cost). If less than one year has passed since the purchase, the gain is taxed as ordinary income; after one year, the gain is currently taxed at 15 percent.

capital loss: The money lost from the sale of an asset or a security.

certificates of deposit (CDs): These follow the federal fund rate and are insured through the Federal Deposit Insurance Corporation (FDIC). For more information, visit www.bankrate.com.

CDSC charges: Back-end load, typically with class B shares. The deferred sales charge can be as high as 6 percent over a declining scale of typically six years.

closed-end fund: A fund that issues a limited number of shares that trade like a stock. Share prices rise and fall with demand and can sell for more or less than its NAV.

commission: A fee charged by brokers (stock brokers, real estate brokers, and so on) for services rendered, such as buying and selling a stock or bond.

commodities: Bulk goods-such as grains, foods, and metals-that are traded on a commodity exchange.

compounding: The growth of interest on the principal plus previously earned interest.

distributions: The payments a fund makes to investors from sales of securities held in the fund, interest, and dividends. It equals the fund's return (or loss) to shareholders. Typically, the fund companies reissue additional shares versus cash distributions.

expense ratio: The charge you pay for your total investment, including management fees, operating expenses, trading costs, sales charges. Check out the average cost and history of funds at www.andrewtobias.com, www.personalfund.com, and www.morningstar.com.

fill or kill: An instruction to cancel the order if it is not executed immediately.

front-end load: An up-front sales charge (commission) to your mutual fund. Sales charges vary from 3.5 percent and up; this is in addition to manager fees, redemption fees, distribution fees, taxes, and any 12b-1 fees the fund may charge.

futures contract: An agreement to purchase or sell a commodity or security at a predetermined price and date.

good-'til-canceled (GTC): Orders that are in effect until executed.

index fund: A fund that imitates the performance of a stock index, such as the S&P 500.

inflation: An increase in the price of goods and services passed on to the consumer.

insider trading: The buying or selling of stock by anyone who has nonpublic information (information not released to the public) that could affect the price of the security.

institutional investor: An organization-such as a bank, mutual fund company, insurance company, pension fund, or money manager-that buys large volumes of securities.

IPO: Initial public offering of a company's stock.

insurance: A contract with an insurance company in which the company agrees to pay a dollar amount for death or disability to an estate or individual in exchange for premiums (dollars).

interest rate: The cost of borrowing money.

investment objective: All funds must have an investment objective-income, growth, balanced, and so on. The objective must be stated in the prospectus.

margin: Borrowing money against a security such as stocks, bonds, or mutual funds.

mortgage rates: Generally tied to ten-year treasury bonds. Adjustable-rate mortgages, home equity lines, and credit lines follow the prime rate.

net asset value: The closing price of each trading day by taking the total value, subtracting expenses, and dividing by the total number of shares outstanding.

open-end fund: A fund that continually issues more shares.

par value: The face value of a bond ($1,000) that can be redeemed or called at par.

P/E ratio: The price of a stock divided by the earnings per share.

pension: A fund established by an employer to provide a set amount of income when an employee retires.

prospectus: The official document describing a mutual fund. It must accompany any sales offering to a client prior to or within a reasonable time period before purchase of the shares.

proxy: An authorized individual who votes on specific agendas of a company. Shareholders are issued proxies.

redemption fee: A charge that may be applied to liquidation of shares held for a short period of time. B or C shares typically carry redemption fees.

short selling: The process of an investor borrowing shares of stock from a broker and hoping the stock will drop in price. The investor buys shares of the same stock when it drops and replaces the borrowed shares for a profit.

stock split: A company splits its stock (generally two for one) to attract more investors, and then hopes the value of the company appreciates. If the stock price was $100 per share and it split two for one, the new price would be $50 per share.

spread: The difference between the bid and offer price of a security.

Securities Investors Protection Corporation (SIPC): The organization that insures brokerage assets (generally $100,000 in cash, $400,000 in securities). Most brokerage houses offer additional insurance protection in case of default.

triple witching day: The third Friday in March, June, September, and December. This is when options, index options, and futures contracts expire at the same time.

zero coupon bond: A bond that is sold at a deep discount and pays no interest. The holder collects the full face value of the bond at maturity.

Notes

Take control, understand your investments, create an estate plan, create a comprehensive budget to show your net cash flow and net worth, and create a retirement budget—all in an easy-to-read fill in the blank format—and *all in one book!*

This book includes the following topics:

A comprehensive mutual fund checklist

Working and retirement budget worksheets

Personal/estate worksheets

Explanations of mutual funds, ETFs, annuities, funds of funds, hedge funds, options, managed money, and more

How to calculate your risk assessment and find your financial DNA

A whole section for bond lovers

Using stop-loss and limit orders to protect your profits

How to choose an adviser

Information on types of mortgages including reverse mortgages, ARM's, and interest only

Mortgage shopping worksheet & checklist

Long-term-health care policies, Medicare, Medicaid, nursing home care, and Web sites

How to register fraud alert...*and a whole lot more*

It is up to you to protect you and your family's financial future. Whether investing or planning your estate, the more you learn, the more you earn—and the more you keep what you earn!

Watch for my next books, *The 401(k) Marketplace, ERISA, DOL, and You: An Essential Guide for Small and Mid-Size Businesses.*

The Procrastinator's Bible for Financial Success: Children and Young Adults